C. L. McPherson

THE UNIVERSITY OF CHICAGO PRESS, CHICAGO
THE BAKER & TAYLOR CO., NEW YORK; THE MACMILLAN COMPANY OF
CANADA, LIMITED, TORONTO; THE CAMBRIDGE UNIVERSITY PRESS,
LONDON; THE MARUZEN-KABUSHIKI-KAISHA, TOKYO, OSAKA, KYOTO,
FUKUOKA, SENDAI; THE COMMERCIAL PRESS, LIMITED, SHANGHAI

THE CHANGING COLLEGE

By
ERNEST HATCH WILKINS
President of Oberlin College

THE UNIVERSITY OF CHICAGO
PRESS · CHICAGO · ILLINOIS

COPYRIGHT 1927 BY THE UNIVERSITY OF CHICAGO.
ALL RIGHTS RESERVED. PUBLISHED NOVEMBER, 1927

COMPOSED AND PRINTED BY THE UNIVERSITY
OF CHICAGO PRESS, CHICAGO, ILLINOIS, U.S.A.

TO MY WIFE

PREFACE

The essays and addresses gathered in this book reflect various phases of my experience as Dean of the Colleges of Arts, Literature, and Science of the University of Chicago during the years 1923 to 1926, and express various elements of my present educational belief, as developed largely through that experience.

Several of these papers have been published elsewhere, and are here reprinted by permission. References to earlier forms of publication and some related matters are embodied in a Note at the end of the book.

E. H. W.

July 30, 1927

TABLE OF CONTENTS

		PAGE
I.	The Changing College	1
II.	The College Curriculum	15
III.	College Teaching	48
IV.	Who Shall Go to College?	73
V.	An Incident in Freshman Registration	84
VI.	Freshman Week	88
VII.	Faculty-Student Co-operation	96
VIII.	The College Bookstore	108
IX.	Intercollegiate Football	114
Note		131

I

THE CHANGING COLLEGE

The edition of the *Encyclopaedia Britannica* which held the shelves until 1910 referred to Amherst College as an institution engaged in "educating poor and pious young men for the ministry." Neither indigence nor the ministerial aim was unknown to the Amherst of 1910—nor are they unknown now—but the *Britannica's* description, once true, had long since become grotesque.

In the perspective of a century, collegiate change stands insistently revealed. We are slow to recognize it in a shorter period—not only slow, but, as alumni, reluctant. Surely the college that produced *us* was an ultimate institution, not to be improved by newcomers' tinkering!

Yet the college, as a living organism, is in constant change. There lie before it, I believe, in the decades soon to come, modifications which will transform it fundamentally. And there are now in process many movements, significant for the future, which have the special interest of contemporaneity.

I

The freshman of today faces a college, and beyond that a world, infinitely more complex than the college and the world of the older generation. We drove our mental wagon along a country road—the youngsters are speeding through city traffic. So much more is known, and there is so much more that we need to know! The older sciences have been fecund in discovery; new sciences are eagerly bringing their contributions. The "branches of knowledge" intertwine in a most amazing way; education is entangled as never before with the other activities of life. There is no isolation, by distance, by time, or by speech. The modern ivory tower is equipped with a superheterodyne.

How shall we light the student through the maze of electives? How fit him to see life whole in this ever more pressing and more difficult world?

A recent and promising device for the partial meeting of this need is the orientation course. I refer not to the series of talks, long in vogue at some institutions, which are intended to acquaint the freshman with the technique of college life—talks about methods of study, the use of the library, the care of health, and so forth—but to a special type of full-time course which instead of dealing with one particular departmental field seeks to survey and to link together the fundamental facts of life in its evolution and in its present human organization.

The first of these courses was that introduced in Amherst, in 1914, on "Social and Economic Institutions." The two which have had widest influence are Columbia's "Introduction to Contemporary Civilization" and Dartmouth's "Evolution," both established in 1919. In 1922 Committee G of the American Association of University Professors brought out a report containing a survey of all the orientation courses then known to be in existence, together with definite recommendations; and the dissemination of this report has been followed by the introduction of orientation courses in many other colleges and universities.

Committee G recommends the division of the orientation program into two sections: the first tracing the story of life from the origin of the earth up to the point where man is defined as man, and covering in general the fields of the physical sciences; the second dealing with the main achievements and the main present problems of man as man, and covering in general the humanistic fields. To these two sections correspond two courses: the first on "The Nature of the World and of Man," to be given in the freshman year; the second on "Man in Society," to be given in the sophomore year. This plan is now followed exactly at the University of Chicago—with the addition of a third and similar course on "The Meaning and Value of the Arts—and the general project thus outlined has been adopted without essential change in several other institutions.

These courses represent a courageous attempt to achieve a modern educational synthesis—to repossess the tremendously enlarged province of all knowledge. I venture to prophesy that a still greater courage—developed perhaps by these very courses—will eventually base an entire freshman and sophomore curriculum upon the principle of orientation.

But it is not enough to know one's world—one must be able to deal with it. We must therefore refine and exercise the instrument of thought.

We have always said that one of the purposes of college was to teach the student how to think—and we have in general let it go at that, believing that some subjects (especially our own) have an inherent disciplinary value, and hoping that exposure to the thought-processes of the faculty would induce a like swiftness and precision in the undergraduate mind. Every college course, indeed, should have training in thought as one of its conscious purposes; but the college of today is beginning to experiment also with training in thought as a separate and specific project.

We have thus a second type of initiatory course, less general than the other as yet, devoted to this purpose. Johns Hopkins and Columbia each introduced such a course in 1921. The

Hopkins course, intended for freshmen, is called "Introduction to College Work"; the Columbia course, a free elective, is called "An Introduction to Reflective Thinking." Chicago now offers a similar course, under the title "Reflective Thinking," to the students who have already had "The Nature of the World and of Man" and are still to have "Man in Society."

II

The freshman and sophomore years are potentially, and to an increasing extent are actually, years of orientation. The junior and senior years are years primarily of concentration. This tenet has been generally accepted since our emergence from elective chaos, and has led to one form or another of departmental or divisional specialization.

Dissatisfaction with the work of the upper years has focused of late not on the principle, but on the manner of concentration. It has been felt that within a chosen field the student is still simply "taking courses," and that he often fails to integrate such departmental knowledge as he thus obtains. The end of his college career too often witnesses not the control of an active body of related information, but a mere collection of grades, every one of which is a *hic jacet*.

There has developed consequently a movement tending to substitute mastery of a subject for the completion of individual course requirements. And the sign and specific method of this movement is the establishment of the general final examination in the major study.

This method involves the requirement that all students concentrating in a given field shall before graduation take a general final examination upon that field, and that this examination shall cover not only those portions of the field which have been studied in particular courses, but also other portions studied through private or directed reading; and furthermore that it shall test a student's ability to perceive and utilize the interrelations of the several particular lines of study.

Bowdoin, Mount Holyoke, Princeton, Reed, and Whitman require such a final examination of all seniors. Harvard requires it of all except those majoring in mathematics or the physical sciences. The universities of California and Washington each require it in two departments.

Concomitant, in theory, to the use of the general final examination is the employment of a staff of tutors or preceptors whose duty it is to prepare students for the examination—and, more generally, to help them win the desired mastery in the chosen field.

Harvard is the only institution whose practice conforms fully to this theory. There are now at Harvard fifty or more men serving as tutors. Some of them devote all their time to this work; others are members of the regular teaching staff, of all ranks from instructor to full professor. Tutorial instruction is given for the most part in individual conferences lasting an hour or less. Sometimes students having a similar interest meet with the teacher in small groups. The University of Washington makes a similar but very limited use of tutors. The other institutions concerned approach a tutorial system less completely. Some have periodic conferences, optional or required, with designated members of the faculty; others rely on student initiative and unorganized faculty helpfulness to solve the problem.

III

The special development of the ablest students is a new and a major concern of the college of today. Society supports the college, in the last analysis, because society looks to the college for the leaders it so greatly needs. Surely, then, the college owes it to society to devote care and energy primarily to those students who give the highest promise of eventual leadership. Any boy or girl once admitted to college deserves sympathetic individual consideration; but the whole surplus of instructional and administrative energy should go to those through whom good seed will bear best fruit. The professor or the dean who incurs exhaustion through soft-hearted or soft-brained surrender to the plights of the "weaker brethren" is in reality disloyal to his task. We should have special advisers for those who are below standard, to help them stay if they should stay, to give them wise and friendly guidance if they should go; but the rest of us should be free to give where the giving will count most. This is not undemocratic—it is of the essence of intelligent and resolute democracy.

The increasing recognition of the special rights of the ablest students is manifesting itself in various ways, some old, some new—through the waiving of ordinary regulations, through rewards and privileges, through invitation courses, through individual hospitality. Most notable of all, just now, are two definite movements in this direction: the practice of sectioning on the basis of ability, and the establishment of honors courses.

Sectioning on the basis of ability is a device appropriate chiefly to the freshman and the sophomore years, for it is possible only when a course has two or more sections meeting at the same hour.

Some division of students must be made in such a case. The division may be purely haphazard, or it may be alphabetical—which is just as bad—or it may be so utilized as to bring together in each section a group of students who are intellectually homogeneous: the ablest students, if there be three sections, in one group; those of medium ability in the second; those of lowest ability in the third. Such an arrangement makes it possible to teach each group to the best advantage. The lowest group may receive all the drill and repetition and explanation it needs, and its members do not suffer by daily contrast with their more brilliant fellows. In the highest group, on the other hand, the ordinary procedure of the classroom may give way in large measure to informal discussion, and there is no loss of time or morale as the result of the slowness of the less able students. It is because of its benefit to the ablest students that the plan has greatest merit; but it works to the advantage of the other groups as well. Every student is kept at his highest level of achievement. Where this plan is thoroughly carried out, provision is made for the periodic transfer of students from a lower to a higher or from a higher to a lower section if the quality of their work indicates that such transfer is desirable.

IV

The honors course is for the junior and senior years the logical continuant of sectioning on the basis of ability in the first two years. It represents a final grouping of students who have distinguished themselves in the first half of their college work.

The honors course is in a sense a special variety, designed for the ablest students, of the plan of the general final examination in the field of concentration. Like that plan, it contemplates mastery of a subject as against the fulfilment of routine course requirements; and like that plan it calls naturally for the development of tutorial assistance, formal or informal. It differs from that plan in that it asks a higher degree of initial qualification and of final achievement; in that it gives a greater independence to the individual student; and in that it requires work additional to or other than that done by the ordinary student.

With respect to this last requirement, honors courses fall into two groups: first, those which involve simply an addition to the regular work, or a substitution of honors work for a relatively small part of the regular work; second, those which involve a substitution of honors work for all or at least for the greater part of the regular work. The line of division is, of course, not absolute.

The development of honors courses of the second type, and in particular of those in which the substitution of special for regular work is nearly or quite complete, is due ultimately to study of the honors systems of Oxford and Cambridge, and has been sponsored in this country very largely by the returned Rhodes Scholars, under the leadership of President Aydelotte.

Harvard, Smith, and Swarthmore are among the institutions in which the idea of the honors course has been most thoroughly developed. At Harvard the term "honors course" is not officially used; but the plan for obtaining the degree with distinction is virtually the same as the plan of the honors course, though there is less release from the ordinary requirements than at some other institutions. At Harvard the system is more completely supported by tutorial guidance than is the case elsewhere. The Swarthmore plan, in which the release from ordinary requirements is complete, is set forth in the following compact statement:

Honors students are excused from the ordinary examinations and course requirements. Instead, they are expected to spend two years in mastering a certain definitely outlined field of knowledge over which they are examined at the end of their two years' work. Their instruction is mainly individual, and a large part of their work is done independently by their own reading. It is open to honors students to attend as many or as few of the regular classes of the college as they desire, though they are guided in this respect by the advice of the Chairman of the division in which they are reading. The comprehensive examinations at the end of their course consist of from ten to twelve three-hour papers followed by an oral examination. These tests are conducted not by the persons who have had charge of the preparation of the candidates, but by professors from other institutions.

The two principles underlying the honors course, according to President Aydelotte, are, first, "the frank distinction between students who are really interested in the intellectual life and those who are not"; and second, "the recognition of the necessity of allowing these better students more responsibility for working out their own intellectual salvation."

V

The orientation course, the course in thinking, the general final examination in the major study, sectioning on the basis of ability, and the honors course seem to me on the whole the most significant of the movements which are working change in the college of today. But there are many other new tendencies and new devices of more or less importance and interest. Some of these I should like to mention with the briefest of comment.

Concern for the student as an individual, long obscured and made well-nigh impossible by the sudden increase in registration in the last few years, is coming to the fore again, reinforced by an enlargement of the administrative staff and by the introduction of various forms of recently developed personnel technique.

Co-operation between faculty and students in the study of various problems of college life and work is being tried, notably at Chicago, with results which lead me to believe that the idea is far richer in educational possibilities than we had ever supposed.

Freshman Week—a contribution of the University of Maine—is helping to adjust the freshman to the college environment in his first critical days of homelessness and bewildering novelty.

Tests are being modernized. We are increasingly better able to ascertain what a student has it in him to do; and in the measurement of what he has done we are trying to test his real achievement rather than his memory.

Faculty members are devoting more time than of old to extra-collegiate enterprises, in research on the behalf of industry, or in the service of city or state. Under right conditions such activity tends to vivify and broaden teaching itself.

Efforts are under way to encourage general reading on the part of undergraduates—reading for its own sake, not necessarily in connection with the special types of independent work referred to above.

Many institutions are seeking in various ways to develop and maintain educational relations with their alumni. There is no inherent reason why the college, which has sought to give an intensive education through four plastic years, should not continue, by pamphlets, reading lists, home study, conferences, or otherwise, to remind the alumni that education is both a matter for life and a vital matter. If such a relationship can be established from the time of graduation, we shall ultimately have a body of alumni much more in sympathy with the real purpose of the college than are alumni of the present day. And alumni groups, even now, are far more readily and genuinely interested in strictly educational matters than the conventional after-dinner speaker seems to suspect.

THE CHANGING COLLEGE

The college is changing, rapidly and profoundly. Yet it remains constant in its intention not merely to perpetuate, but to learn and to serve. And it remains constant in the certainty that methods and devices, invaluable though they be for the release and the direction of power, are but the instruments of that power which lies, in the last analysis, in the warmth and light of devoted intellectual personality.

II

THE COLLEGE CURRICULUM

Through college gates throng boys and girls in the glow of youth, possessed in goodly measure of the fundamentally human "desire to know," quickly responsive to the call of the ideal. Through four plastic years the college holds them in trust. If that trust be well fulfilled they will go forth, men and women, established in health and strength, trained in mind, and glad to play their loyal parts in the great drama of life. If that trust be not well fulfilled they will fall short of their potential leadership —or they will use to the harm of society the forces they have learned to control.

The central purpose of the college is the training of the minds of its students. This training is twofold: it involves, first, the acquisition of knowledge by the student, and, second, training in the processes of the acquisition and the use of knowledge.

The modern man needs two types of knowledge. If he is to be a sympathetic, broad-minded, and generally intelligent member of society he should have some measure of significant and ordered knowledge of each of the main fields of human interest. The late President Ernest D. Burton said:

> A college ought to enable all its students to place themselves in the world, to recognize where they are. It ought to help each student to acquire such a knowledge of the physical universe, of the history of the race, of the structure of society, and of the nature of the individual that, taking his stand at the center of his own being, he may have a sense of where he is.[1]

And if the modern man is to render efficient individual service in the maintenance and development of human society, he must have a large measure of significant and ordered knowledge within some special field. College education should, therefore, be in part general, in part special—in part extensive, in part intensive.

The vision of this dual need has been the torch which has led the college out of the elective chaos. The two objectives are now recognized in every well-organized curricular system. Nomenclature varies. With reference to the first objective such terms as "general education," "orientation," and "distribution" are in common use; with reference to the second, "special education," the "major study," and "concentration."

---

[1] "The Business of a College," in *Education in a Democratic World* (Chicago, 1927), pp. 62–63.

Broadly speaking, the process of general education is now chiefly associated with the first two years of the college course, and the process of special education with the last two years. There is, however, no line of absolute division. Relatively intensive work in a single field is often begun before the midpoint of the course; and general education claims as large a share of the last two years as the increasing specialization will allow.

Current American practice, then, divides the college curriculum of the individual student about equally between general and special education, general education being emphasized in the first two years and special education in the last two years. This practice appears to be sound, at least under present conditions.

General education, as has been said, implies the attainment of some measure of significant and ordered knowledge of each of the main fields of human interest. Let us now consider in some detail the implications of this statement.

A survey of the subjects taught in a typical college will show the existence of three main groups of subjects, and of certain other subjects not included in the main groups. The three main groups are: the social sciences; the languages, literatures, and arts; and the physical sciences. The order given is the traditional one; it has, however, no logical propriety. Let us place the physical sciences first, leave out the languages for the time being, and let the term "the arts" include literature as well as the other arts. We shall then have this sequence: the physical sciences; the social sciences; the arts.

This new sequence is at once luminous with evolutionary significance. For the physical sciences deal with that which is infra-human and with the human in so far as it partakes of the infra-human; the social sciences deal with man in the relations forced upon him by the conditions of human society; the arts are the free creation of man's surplus super-physical energy.

The physical sciences describe the ever changing stage upon which the human drama is being played; indicate the basic conditions of man's existence; and give to him a swiftly increasing ability to control the dangers and to utilize the opportunities of the infra-human environment.

The social sciences face the central problem —the problem of human behavior. They describe human behavior in many different fields, studying motives, methods, and results; and they seek ultimately to inform man as to the effects of various kinds of action, in order that he may adapt himself to his companions and with them work out a way of living which shall yield to each as great a measure of fulness of life as the fundamental conditions of existence will permit.

The arts are of a different order. They are, in the long evolutionary perspective, something new—a social increment. They are themselves means for the enlargement of life—products and reservoirs of surplus energy, perennially ready, with due mediation, to pour their treasure into new lives.

Such, in broadest outline, are the three main groups of subjects. General education obviously calls for a very considerable amount of study within each of these three groups.

Let us now examine these groups more closely, considering the subdivisions of each, and taking up, at the appropriate points, the subjects not included in the main groups.

The physical sciences include the two basic physical sciences, physics and chemistry; the two sciences concerned with the observation of the inorganic universe, astronomy and geology; and the biological sciences, which in turn include the infra-human biological sciences, botany and zoölogy, and the main human biological sciences, anatomy and physiology.

Between the physical and the social groups are three sciences, geography, hygiene, and psychology, which are in part physical and in part social. Geography deals, to be sure, with the infra-human earth, but modern geography deals more and more constantly and intently with the earth as the home of human life—geography is indeed becoming human ecology. Hygiene, growing out of the biological sciences, deals with the physical welfare of man as affected primarily by his human environment.

Psychology, historically an offshoot of philosophy, is striking root more and more deeply in the soil of physiology.

The social sciences, strictly so called, are three: sociology, the general science of human ways of living; economics, the special science which deals with the socialized provision of the material and the conditions requisite for the preservation and maintenance of life; and political science, the special science which deals with the generalized means of social control.

Closely related to the social sciences are three fields of study of a somewhat different character: history, which is concerned with the entire human past; philosophy, which is concerned, as metaphysics, with the synthetic interpretation of the results of all types of observation, and, as ethics, with the very heart of the whole problem of conduct; and religion, which, as a field of study, is properly concerned with the whole range of religious experience, belief, and organization, past and present.

Of the arts, literature alone is universally present in the college list of subjects. By the force of tradition, by its very extensiveness, and by its inherent values, it affirms itself therein in many local and temporal varieties, which fall into two main groups: the English and American literatures, and the foreign literatures. Literature in one of its main aspects is closely allied to the social sciences, for it is the chief medium whereby the phenomena of human experience which seem significant to a human group in one time and place are passed on to human groups in other times and other places.

The other arts, music, architecture, sculpture, and painting, are steadily gaining recognition as rightful fields of college study—for they, though in lesser measure than literature, carry the message of man to man, and they, even more directly than literature, make for the enlargement of life.

There remain certain subjects which, unlike the foregoing, are not primarily—for the college student—fields for the acquisition of knowledge, but are rather means of training in the processes of the acquisition and the use of knowledge. They may be classed, roughly, as general mental tools. They are mathematics, logic, English, and the several foreign languages. Mathematics underlies and makes possible all true science, physical or social; and logic, less formal than of yore, is still its companion. The languages, to the college student, are primarily significant as media of understanding and utterance within the fields both of science and of literature. English is of course of primary importance.

The classification of subjects thus suggested is illustrated by the table on the next page.

Truly the man who would now take all knowledge to be his province faces a task impossible! And yet if the modern man is to be an intelligent dweller in this increasingly complex world he can hardly afford totally to neglect any one of the physical or physical-social sciences listed above; if he is to live and work effectively and companionably with other men he can hardly afford totally to neglect any one of the social or physical-social sciences; and

TABULAR SURVEY OF THE FIELD OF GENERAL EDUCATION

Physical Sciences	Physical-Social Sciences	Social Sciences	Studies Closely Related to the Social Sciences	Arts	General Mental Tools
Physics Chemistry Astronomy Geology Botany Zoölogy Anatomy Physiology	Geography Hygiene Psychology	Sociology Economics Political Science	History Philosophy Metaphysics Ethics Religion	Literature English and American Foreign Music Architecture Sculpture Painting	Mathematics Logic English Foreign Language

if he seeks enlargement of life for himself and for his intimates he can hardly afford totally to neglect any one of the several arts. If he would understand the human past and present, and fully participate in the life of his own generation, he can hardly neglect history, or philosophy, or religion. If he is to be effective in thought and speech, he can hardly neglect mathematics or logic or English. If he would avoid provinciality, he can hardly dispense with the knowledge of at least one foreign language.

Only half of the college curriculum, or thereabouts, is to be devoted to general education. Obviously the student cannot within two years' space gain an adequate measure of even general acquaintance with the vast field of knowledge outlined above. Furthermore, many of the subjects mentioned are such that a good general acquaintance with them may be won by students of pre-college age. Obviously, therefore, the process of general education should begin long before the student comes to college. It is indeed only by the careful interweaving of the high-school curriculum and part of the college curriculum that a satisfactory program of general education can be achieved.

The present inquiry, however, is concerned with the college curriculum. The immediate problem is therefore this: assuming that each freshman comes to college with the process of general education begun but incomplete, what curricular provision shall be made for the completion of the process?

The natural collegiate method of gaining knowledge in a given field is to take a course or courses in that field. And for the purpose of meeting the need in this way, every department should offer a single course, or a short sequence of courses, intended to give some measure of significant and ordered knowledge to the student who takes work in the department solely as a phase of his general education, and has no intention of specializing in the field in question.

But no student can take or should take anything like the whole set of such courses and course-sequences. Clearly, then, a choice must be made. On what principles? Four, I believe: the principle of adaptation to individual need; the principle of major significance; the principle of group representation; and the principle of integration.

The word "curriculum" has no proper modern significance except as designating a course of study created anew for each individual student. No two students bring to college the same background, the same experience, the same achievement in knowledge; and no two students face the same future of work and of leisure. We have no right to do less than to study with the utmost care each individual record and each individual prospect, and to plan the individual curriculum in accordance with the results of that study.

Study of the individual record involves study of the whole previous experience of the student—particularly, of course, his high-school work. Such study should not be limited to ascertainment of the fact that he has taken certain subjects, but should include an estimation of the extent to which each phase of his work has entered into the structure of his mental life. The results of this study should be checked with the list of the several subjects together constituting the field of general education as defined above. In certain subjects, it will appear that the student has already a considerable measure of ordered and significant knowledge of the special field in question. Such subjects may, therefore, be omitted from the student's college program of general education. In the other subjects, it will appear that the student's knowledge is quite negligible, or at least inadequate. In some such cases, but not in all, he should take introductory courses, or short course-sequences, in the fields in question; and in the selection of these courses he should be guided by the principles of major significance and of group representation. In other cases he should gain or develop knowledge through one of the means of integration to be suggested below.

To the principle of adaptation to individual need I shall revert in another connection. I turn now to the principle of major significance.

Are there, among the subjects listed, any of such outstanding significance that they should certainly appear in the typical individual curriculum? My answer is, distinctly, "Yes." And the subjects I should designate—with full recognition of the fact that there is room for difference of opinion in this matter—are hygiene, psychology, logic, and English.

Such knowledge of hygiene as a college course in personal and social hygiene could and should give is fundamentally necessary as one of the means for the building and maintenance of the type of healthy body which alone can stand the exhausting strain of real leadership and alone can pulsate with the magnetism which effective leadership requires. The study of hygiene has, therefore, a direct part in physical as well as in mental training. Moreover, in the community life which the college graduate is to enter, no single practical contribution is more needed than that of the intelligent initiation and support of measures concerning the hygienic welfare of the community as a whole.

Psychology is, to my mind, the key-subject in the modern intellectual advance. Every one of the social sciences, together with philosophy and religion, is realizing more and more closely that it cannot reach valid and significant conclusions with regard to conduct without such understanding of the normal processes of the complete human being as psychology seeks to give. Ultimately no conduct-sanction will endure which is not established on psychological foundations. There is, therefore, pressing need for the right building of these foundations. For these reasons I advocate giving to every college student some measure of acquaintance with the psychological field, so that if he shows the least sign of special ability therein he may be encouraged, for the sake of society, to develop that ability. And I make this recommendation with full recognition of the fact—all the more urgently because of the fact—that psychology is still in the stage of groping infancy.

The college student is not only to acquire various types of knowledge; he is to be trained in the methods of acquiring and using knowledge. The main instrument for this training is logic—logic of the modern inductive type, case-system logic. We have always said that one of the main tasks of the college is to teach the student how to think; but we have left the fulfilment of that task to each other, or to chance, on the supposition, apparently, that exposure to the processes of the professorial mind as revealed in the general run of college courses would through imitation produce a like logical perfection in student minds. True it is that every college course should have as a definite secondary purpose the training of the student in the methods of thought within a particular field; but we fall short of our duty if we do not make a specific and concentrated effort, while the student is with us, to see and to let him see how he actually reasons, to correct and improve his mental processes just so far as that may be possible, and to develop his mind as nearly as we can to the greatest efficiency of which it is inherently capable.

The best means thus far found for the making of such an effort is the course in logic of the type of the Johns Hopkins "Introduction to College Work" and of the Columbia and Chicago "Introduction to Reflective Thinking."

The proposition that the study of English is of major importance should need no argument. Effective utterance, both written and oral, is necessary for effective leadership. Even clarity in thinking is very largely dependent upon the habit of clarity in expression. And the stage of general education in English is not passed, no matter how many courses may have been taken, until the student is able to express clearly and agreeably whatever he has to say. Training in English, like training in logic, should be, so far as possible, individualized. It may not even take course form. It is not likely to be well achieved through the mass production of themes from an artificially created mental vacuum.

Psychology and logic are specifically college subjects—so also is hygiene as here conceived. A few students reach the desired proficiency in English before coming to college. For them, therefore, collegiate training in English is unnecessary.

Since training in respect to the general attitude toward life is a proper and vital part of college training, it might seem that ethics, which is directly concerned with the development of right attitudes, should be added to the list of subjects of major significance. Every care should indeed be taken that the instruction in ethics should be both able and attractive. But the very spirit of modern ethics lies in the substitution of inner for outer sanctions; it would, therefore, be peculiarly unfortunate that such a course should be handicapped by being put upon a required basis. And no course in ethics, however effective, could carry the full responsibility for ethical training. That responsibility rests upon the entire faculty, and is best to be fulfilled not by indoctrination but by honorable and serviceable living.

The student, then, is to be exempt from further study of subjects adequately covered in the high school, and is presumably to be required to take work in hygiene, psychology, logic, and, in most cases, English. The curricular time available for the rounding out of his general knowledge is not nearly enough—even supposing him to have had a better than average high-school experience—to enable him to take courses in each of the many fields which are as yet quite new or but slightly familiar to him. How, then, shall he choose? The principle next to be invoked is that of group representation.

Inspection of the field of general education as outlined and tabulated above shows at once the existence of certain natural groups of specific subjects. Thus, within the division of physical sciences appear these groups: (*a*) the basic physical sciences; (*b*) the sciences concerned with the observation of the inorganic universe; and (*c*) the biological sciences. Moreover, each of the subjects which stand outside these natural groups is sufficiently relevant to some other subject or subjects to be regarded as forming a group therewith. Thus the whole field—omitting the four subjects of major significance—may be regarded as divisible into the following groups: (1) mathematics, physics, chemistry; (2) astronomy, geology, geography; (3) the biological sciences; (4) sociology, history; (5) economics, political science; (6) philosophy, religion; (7) the literatures; (8) architecture, sculpture, painting, music; and (9) the foreign languages. I do not maintain that this grouping is inevitable; it is intended to serve as a possible typical plan.

General education obviously calls for a considerable amount of study within each of the larger divisions of the field of general education. The specific principle of group representation, a logical development of that obvious general principle, indicates that one course or short course-sequence should be taken (unless the field has already been adequately represented in the student's high-school work) in each group of a series such as that just suggested.

Application of the foregoing principles will still leave some subjects untouched, and will accentuate the need for some synthesis of the several types of knowledge with which the student has become and is becoming acquainted. How shall he gain some significant idea of the fields within which he cannot take a course? How shall he assemble his blocks of disparate information into a significant and ordered whole?

Just here, to my mind, lies the permanent function of the general survey or "orientation" courses which have come recently into such wide vogue. Their initial function has been to assert the need for a synthetic view of the whole collegiate field and to provide an opportunity for such a view pending the organization of a plan of general education which would meet the need with some degree of adequacy. They have served hitherto to furnish a general suggestion of what is going on in the physical and social sciences to students in whose experience whole ranges of human interest might otherwise have been left blank. They have been carrying the primary burden in the endeavor to acquaint the student systematically with his universe and with his fellow man. But just in so far as the present disorganized election of courses is superseded by an organized plan of general education the burden upon the general survey courses will be diminished. With such a plan in operation, however, the general survey courses will still retain the double purpose of giving the student some touch with the fields in which he has not taken and is not expecting to take courses, and of establishing a synthetic perspective control of the whole territory of intellectual life. They will thus be, in a double sense, courses of integration.

The normal place for courses having this double purpose is at the end of the period devoted primarily to general education—that is, in the sophomore year. There should be three such courses, running in sequence throughout the year. The first should deal with the physical and the physical-social sciences; the second with the social sciences, history, philosophy, and religion; and the third with the arts.

Survey courses in the first two of these fields are now given in many colleges. The University of Chicago is, so far as I know, the only institution providing the full triple series.

The method of these courses should be determined in accordance with the answer given by the organizer to these two questions: "How shall I best give the students some initiation into the several fields which they have not touched hitherto?" and "How shall I lead them to bring together into an ordered whole the stocks of information and of interest which they have gained or are gaining in other courses, in this course, or elsewhere?"

The twofold purpose of the course creates a special problem in organization. During each portion of the course the student personnel will comprise both students who have already covered the subject in question and students to whom that subject is new. The composition of the two groups will shift as the course reaches each new field. Clearly the same treatment will not be adapted for both groups. The situation will best be met by dividing the course, for each of the different portions, into two sections, one for each of the two groups, the sectioning changing as the course enters each new field. In the section consisting of those who have already studied the subject in question the paramount purpose will be that of emphasizing the synthetic significance of the subject, particularly its relationship with adjacent subjects. Differential programs of collateral work may readily be planned. Books which themselves interweave results or theories in different fields may be of particular value in this connection. Students in the experienced section may be used to some extent as helpers in the initiation of students who are in the inexperienced section.

A third purpose, which is in reality a special phase of the first, is the renovation at the sophomore level of the student's acquaintance with subjects which he has studied in high school but not in college.

Each of the three courses should be something more than a series of descriptions of related subjects; each should be given coherence and vitality by some specific inner character. For the course in the physical sciences this inner character is quite obviously afforded by the concept of evolution. For the course in the social sciences the same concept may be continued, or, since the problem here is that of conduct, the course may proceed by the discussion of current problems, involving individual or group conduct, in the several fields considered. For the course in the arts, while the evolutionary background may well be recognized, the specific purpose should be to give each student a chance to realize something of the enrichment of life that lies for him in acquaintance with the works of art, the music and the literature available to him; and to render each student more sensitive to the values, in life itself, which form the data of artistic re-creation.

A second means of integration, necessary if general survey courses are for any reason not given, and in some cases desirable per se, is self-initiation into a given field through independent reading of the best initiatory books. I shall turn in a moment to the question of general reading. My present suggestion is that a good student may well be encouraged to enter alone some field quite new to him—alone, that is, in companionship with the thought of able writers. Current collegiate experience still tends all too much to give the impression that the only way to gain knowledge of a subject is to take a course in it. We are seeking not only to see that our students get knowledge, but also to train them in the acquisition of knowledge. The formation of the habit of the acquisition of knowledge through the independent use of books is a major factor in this training—and if this habit is not formed in college it is not likely ever to be formed.

We have made great progress, within the limits of the individual course, in the use of books rather than of lectures for the gaining of certain bodies of information. But the practice of discovery through independent reading should be still further emphasized and given still further scope. I therefore strongly recommend that at least one field be covered by the student through private reading; that such reading be regarded by the college as equivalent to course-taking; and that for practical purposes it be duly tested and credited.

Still more important is the development, as a phase of general education, of the habit of general reading. The college experience should be such as to merge gradually into the later experience of life. The process of education in the college should be so devised that it may continue naturally and readily throughout life. The idea that education stops with Commencement is a tragic absurdity. Now the normal means of education in later life—aside, of course, from the more or less haphazard education of personal experience—is the reading of books, particularly current books, and current periodicals. Therefore the habit of the discriminating reading of current books and periodicals should be formed in college. In this instance also, if the habit is not formed in college it is not likely ever to be formed.

Notable interpretations of life, notable suggestions for the betterment of the conditions of life, and notable reviews of significant books are constantly appearing in the weekly and monthly press. Through books themselves come most clearly the significant records of past lives and the voices of our own prophets. Books and periodicals alike bring store for literary satisfaction. And some are good and some are negligible and some are bad. It is true, again, that current books and periodicals are being used more than ever before in connection with particular courses; but it is also true that the greater part of what we call current literature is not likely to be made known to the students through the courses they take. How then shall it be made known to them?

Acquaintance with current literature can hardly be a thing superadded to a curriculum already completely full. There is a limit to the use of eyesight and to the use of the reading faculty. There must be no infringement upon the time needed for recreation and for sleep. The answer is then obviously to reduce the amount of ordinary course work sufficiently to make possible the practice of a considerable amount of general reading. If the course mechanism be necessary, the reading can be done under the aegis of a special course name and number; but it would be better that it should be done in some other way. The library and the librarian should presumably have a major responsibility in this matter—and the college bookstore should be an ally and not an enemy. Guidance is necessary; but the guidance should be suggestive rather than imperative.

This reading is, strictly speaking, quasi-curricular. It should be the main quasi-curricular experience. There are other types of experience which, though secondary, are of the same order. Such, for instance, is the study at first hand of some type of community life and work accessible to the college; and such is the whole range of lectures, dramatic performances, concerts, and exhibitions—too often overdone, too seldom planned with definite reference to the whole process of college growth.

The first two years of the college course, while devoted primarily to general education, should include also some measure of special education—that is, some fairly intensive study of a given field. Such study is indeed a necessary complement to general education as a means of training students in the processes of the acquisition and the use of knowledge. For if the mind is to function effectively in solving the varied and unexpected problems which will confront it throughout life, it must have the experience of striking deeply into one particular range of thought. Without this experience the lesser study of several different fields might tend toward superficiality. Such specialization should not only give some sense of mastery in the chosen field, but should convince the student that only specialization can give mastery in any field, and should establish in him a habit of specialistic achievement transferable to work in other fields.

The specialization of the first two years, however, is preliminary, not final. It does not seek the absolute mastery of a given field as an end in itself; it is concerned with the attainment of the experience of intensive work, and with the establishment of a transferable habit of specialization. Consequently, it may or it may not lie in the field which is to be chosen for the final specialization.

In the case of a student who on entrance does not know what his field of final specialization is to be, the field of preliminary specialization should be chosen, under guidance, with reference to his natural tastes and abilities. If the preliminary specialization should confirm the student in such tastes and abilities, he may very naturally continue in the same field; but if some other interest should develop to a greater power during his first two years, that other interest rather than the first should become the field of his final specialization.

If the student on entrance does know what he is to do after graduation, it does not follow that his preliminary specialization should lie in the line of his vocational intent. The chances are, indeed, that it should lie elsewhere. For the principle of adaptation to the individual need of the student might well mean, in this connection, the development of interests, old or new, outside of the field in which he is to specialize. The development of these non-special interests is a precious thing, likely to add, to that breadth of outlook which the program of general education should in any case provide, a free-ranging, individual eagerness, which should forever prevent undue narrowness and should forever increase a man's value in companionship.

The foregoing pages have developed the belief that the curriculum of the individual student, in so far as his general education is concerned, should be determined with reference to the principles of adaptation to individual need, major significance, group representation, and integration; have suggested orientation courses and independent reading as means of integration; have urged the attempt to create a habit of general reading; and have pointed out the necessity of preliminary specialization as a concomitant of general education. Before we pass on to a consideration of the final specialization proper to the last two years of the college course, it may be well to illustrate in a particular imaginary case the application of what has been said hitherto.

Let us suppose, then, that Harper Eliot comes to college after the completion of a good high-school course; that he has received in the fields of mathematics, physics, geography, history, and French as good a training as the requirements of general education would demand; and that his most marked tastes and abilities are in the field of history. Let us suppose, further, that during his four years in college he is to take three full-time courses through each autumn, winter, and spring—a total of nine courses each year and of thirty-six for his entire college program;[1] that eighteen of these courses are to be devoted to general education, six to preliminary specialization, and twelve to final specialization; that the first two years are to contain twelve of the courses devoted to general education, as well as the six devoted to preliminary specialization; and that the last two years are to contain the remaining six of the courses devoted to general education, as well as the twelve devoted to final specialization.

The principle of adaptation to individual need would suggest on its positive side that young Eliot's preliminary specialization should be in the field of history—thus indicating the subject of the six courses which are to constitute this phase of his education—and on its negative side that there is no need of his taking further courses in mathematics, physics, geography, or a foreign language.

He has now to choose the equivalent of eighteen courses for the completion of his general education. The principle of major significance will account for four of these by its specification of hygiene, psychology, logic, and English. Let us suppose, further, that he shows enough aptitude in psychology to justify his taking two additional courses in that field, and

[1] I am stating the supposed case in terms of the quarter system because I firmly believe in the excellence of that system. Its adaptation to the needs of general education is indeed a main argument in its favor. The illustration may, however, be readily translated into other terms.

that he proves to need two courses in English. Seven of the eighteen courses are thus accounted for.

Reference to the list of groups of subjects will next suggest that he should take an introductory course or course-sequence in each of the following groups: the biological sciences; economics-political science; philosophy-religion; the literatures; architecture-sculpture-painting-music. If he should take a single course in each of four of these groups and a two-course sequence in the fifth (say, economics-political science), he would thus expend six of his remaining eleven courses.

Of the five courses still left, three should be orientation courses. Of the other two, one might well be a course in independent reading devoted to initiation into a literary field otherwise untouched, and the other a course in general reading.

Twelve of the eighteen courses thus selected would come in his freshman and sophomore years. These should include the required courses in hygiene and logic, the first course in psychology, both courses in English, and the three orientation courses—eight in all. The other four might well be the course in the biological sciences, the two-course sequence, and the course in general reading. There would then remain for his junior and senior years two courses in psychology, one in philosophy or religion, one regular course in literature, one reading course in literature, and one course in architecture or sculpture or painting or music.

In tabular form the individual curriculum of Harper Eliot might then appear as follows:

Year	Quarter	Courses in General Education	Courses in Special Education
Freshman	Autumn Winter Spring	English; Botany English; Hygiene Logic; Psychology	History History History
Sophomore	Autumn Winter Spring	Orientation; Economics Orientation; Economics Orientation; General Reading	History History History
Junior	Autumn Winter Spring	Psychology Psychology Literature	Subject of final specialization: two courses each quarter
Senior	Autumn Winter Spring	Architecture Literature (reading) Philosophy	

The foregoing illustration—let me make it quite clear—is intended merely as a study in possibilities. I do not insist upon its proportions, nor upon its distribution in time, nor upon its details. For a student entering with other equipment and with a definite vocational plan, a very different curriculum would be advisable.

Two-thirds, or thereabouts, of the last two years of the college course should be devoted to the student's final specialization. The field of this specialization should be chosen with reference to the interests which are likely to dominate the student's later life.

The present frequent lack of relation be-

THE COLLEGE CURRICULUM 43

tween college experience and ultimate settlement within a given profession or other line of life-work is indeed a deplorable, even a tragic circumstance. Surely every endeavor should be made to utilize the final collegiate specialization in such a way as to qualify the man or woman directly for that which he or she is chiefly to be and to do.

The choice of the final special field is, therefore, a matter of critical importance in the building of the individual curriculum. Here even more than elsewhere the student needs the most patient and the most expert guidance that the college can possibly provide. Preconceived ideas as to vocation may prove on examination to be unwise; and the many students who have as yet no definite life-plan must be helped in the making of reasoned plans. We know all too little as yet about the relationships between certain different characteristics and certain occupations—and this is one of the main arguments for the concentration of effort upon advance in psychological research—but the student is entitled to the advantage of all that we do know.

A man finally resolved to enter a given profession or vocation should certainly choose for his final collegiate specialization the field of his profession itself, if undergraduate work within that field is offered in his college, or a field definitely preparatory for his professional work—chemistry, for instance, if he is going into medicine, or economics if he is going into business.

In the case of a man whose vocational intention is but tentative, the field chosen should presumably be pre-professional rather than professional.

The college woman of today faces a twofold prospect. In the first place, she is likely ultimately to have home-making as a primary or secondary occupation.[1] In the second place, she has or should have some other definite field of interest, which may or may not be vocational. Her final specialization, therefore, should in general be twofold.

Home-making as a vocation is second to none in significance or in difficulty. Yet it is done for the most part without specific preparation, on the basis of family tradition, of individual instinct, and of trial and error. Is there any reason why a woman in college should not prepare for this profession with the utmost care, entering into the stored and swiftly developing knowledge that will help her directly in the many and varied problems of the creation and maintenance of a true home? If there is not, we

[1] Statistics gathered by L. V. Koos with regard to the occupations of 550 woman graduates, representing a dozen different colleges, in the first and tenth years after graduation show that in the first year after graduation 12 per cent were engaged in advanced study, 72 per cent in educational work, 6 per cent in home-making, and 10 per cent in other occupations; and that in the tenth year after graduation 55 per cent of the same women were engaged in home-making, 25 per cent in educational work, and 20 per cent in other occupations (*The Junior College Movement* [Boston, 1925], pp. 208–9).

are driven to the conclusion that for most women, except those definitely resolved to espouse an independent profession, home economics, including the psychology of home relationships, should be at least a secondary field of collegiate specialization.

Yet these same women should have as well some other field, primary or secondary, of special interest. For no reasonable person in this day and generation would think of limiting women's interest to the home, or of denying them full right of access to all human knowledge and experience, or of belittling the immense social need of their participation in the solution of our infinitely serious and complex social problems.

A woman, having thus two fields of specialization, will need somewhat more total time for specialization, particularly if one of her fields be definitely vocational, than a man, who has one field of specialization. The additional time thus necessary may be saved through a lessening of the time spent in general education, or through the partial or complete equation of the preliminary and one of the final fields of specialization.

Many college graduates, both men and women, enter the field of education. Leadership in that field requires a double equipment: knowledge of a particular subject and a general knowledge of educational procedure. The second part of this equipment is all too often neglected—left, like home-making, to individual instinct and to trial and error. This neglect results not only in needlessly poor teaching, but in the failure of the teacher to see as a whole the enterprise of the school or the college in which he lives and works, and in his consequent failure to do his part constructively as colleague in the solution of its common problems. It follows, therefore, that any student intending to teach should supplement his or her special work in a particular subject by courses and by directed reading in the field of education.

When a field of specialization has once been chosen, the control of the individual curriculum should be primarily departmental. The department should have the power not only to advise and in effect to determine what courses the student should take, but to determine the extent to which individual independent work may be encouraged and expected in lieu of course work. The principles here involved are essentially the same as those discussed above in connection with self-initiation into a particular field and in connection with general reading; and the discussion need not be repeated here.

The specific forms in which these principles are now finding expression are the special plan of major work now in effect at Harvard, Princeton, and elsewhere, and the honors course. These plans are treated in the preceding essay.[1]

I have written hitherto in terms of the current four-year college, and without differentiat-

[1] See above, pp. 5-7 and 9-11.

ing the separate four-year college from the liberal arts college within the university. Into the details of the curricular variation natural in different types of collegiate institutions I will not attempt to enter. I should like, however, to suggest that in the college within the university, where large library resources and laboratory equipment are available and graduate or professional schools are at hand, the process of special education should play a relatively larger part than in the separate colleges, which can best render a distinctive service through the prolongation and great development of general education.

The junior college, conceived as a terminal institution, should be devoted almost wholly to general education—with provision, however, for some measure of special education, designed primarily for the establishment of the habit of thorough penetration into a given field.

III

COLLEGE TEACHING

The college exists because society desires that youth be taught. Teaching, then, is the thing primarily expected of the college. Teaching is, moreover, precisely what the college itself most desires to do, most delights in doing, is best qualified to do, and does best.

The modern college has, to be sure, an extraordinary variety of functions; but teaching is by so far the most important that all the others taken together cannot rival it in significance. Many of the other functions are indeed by-products of the teaching. Teaching is, in the last analysis, *the* function of the college.

The quality of the teaching is the measure of the success of the college. If the teaching is good, the college is a good college, even though its plant be inadequate and its athletic stars be dim. If the teaching is poor, the college is a poor college, even though it have a Freshman Week and a psychiatrist. If the teaching is good, the college justifies its existence and deserves encouragement. If the teaching is and remains poor, the college deserves extinction.

Teaching is done by teachers. The essential life of the college is in its faculty; and it is in its teaching that the faculty as such is most alive.

The central concern of all those interested in the vitality of the college—the faculty itself, the administrative officers, the trustees, the alumni, the students, and the whole community, immediate or remote, wherein the light of the college shines—should be that the faculty be composed of good teachers; that the conditions of their work should be such as to facilitate good teaching; and that they should actually teach to the best of their ability.

What constitutes a good teacher?

Take the five or six best teachers you have known; distinguish, if you can, the elements of their power; and combine the recurrent elements in a single composite personality.

When I do so, the visioned figure, poised in the attitude of Charles Edward Garman, looks at me with the eyes of William Lyman Cowles, and speaks and smiles and moves with the attributes of friends who are teaching today.

He knows his subject—this composite teacher—and he believes profoundly in its significance, immediate or ultimate, for the enrichment of human life. He cares about his students, as thinking, feeling, and growing individuals, and is glad to listen to them and to talk to them, in the classroom or outside the classroom. For their sakes, and because of the nature of his own mind, he selects his material rigorously and orders it effectively. His presentation has always some measure of informality, of give and take. He is courteous and helpful to all; but his chief concern is for the stimulation and the guidance of his ablest students. He is a born teacher; but he is a made teacher as well—made through friendly contacts with colleagues in his own college and elsewhere, through deliberate study of the art of teaching within his own field, through the resolute development of his own powers.

The lineaments of your composite teacher will differ inevitably, to some extent, from those of mine; yet the chances are that in my description you have seen a figure closely akin to the one which you evoke.[1]

In the selection of new men or women for the teaching staff, the question first to be asked is surely this: "Is he," or "Is she, a good teacher?" This question should be not only asked but answered; and the answer should be clean-cut and supported by substantial evidence. The matter is so fundamentally important as to

---

[1] Compare President Angell's statement of *desiderata* in the *Report of the President of Yale University* for 1924–25, pp. 11–15. The most discriminating extensive analysis known to me of the qualities of a good teacher is an ordered list of "Qualities Desirable in Instructors in Elementary Courses Conducted by the Lecture-Discussion Method," prepared in 1924 and 1925 by a large joint faculty-student committee at the University of Chicago under the chairmanship of Professor F. S. Breed, and printed and discussed in Professor Breed's article, "A Guide for College Teaching," in *School and Society*, XXIV (1926), 82–87.

justify an expenditure of time and care in the process of selection far beyond that customarily allotted to it. President Hopkins of Wabash College, in his notable study of "Personnel Procedure in Education,"[1] reports that in none of the institutions which he visited did he find a procedure for the selection of instructors which seemed to him a significant contribution to the problem. The trouble is that the persons of whom the question "Is he a good teacher?" is ordinarily asked are all too often unable to give an intelligent answer. How often does the president really know the teaching qualities of his departmental heads? How often do departmental heads really know the teaching qualities of their subordinates? And how often does the head of a university graduate department really know the teaching qualities of his graduate students?

Yet the essence of the matter, from the point of view of proper appointment, lies precisely here. It is true that qualities other than teaching ability are desirable, and it is true that some defect or limitation in respect to such other qualities may serve to veto an appointment; but no possible combination of other qualities, however superlative, can justify the appointment of a poor teacher. What shall it profit a college to add to its teaching staff a man who has a fine voice, is a natural mixer, plays golf in

[1] *Educational Record*, *Supplement*, No. 3 (1926), pp. 66–71.

the eighties, is a tireless and efficient committeeman, a productive scholar, an idealist in life and work—and cannot teach? Teaching is the soul of the enterprise. Unto the teacher these other qualities may well be added; but teaching ability must be there as the basic quality of all.

It is, then, the duty of the president, or of anyone else responsible for an appointment, to use every possible means to ascertain the teaching ability of the candidate he is considering. And it is, I believe, a primary duty owed by administrative officers and departmental heads to the profession at large that they should enable themselves to speak intelligently with regard to the teaching ability of their younger colleagues or their graduate students.

I have neither the wisdom nor the experience to prescribe a set of methods whereby such knowledge may be surely gained; but I believe that some of the procedures in training and in teaching which I shall suggest below will help toward this attainment.[1]

Given a faculty composed of good teachers, the prime responsibility of the college lies in the maintenance and development of their teaching ability.

Maintenance and development of teaching ability involve the continuance or the establishment of good teaching conditions, the con-

---

[1] The principle of the primacy of the teaching function should apply with similar force in the difficult problems of promotion and of retirement.

stant revitalizing of the mind, and the provision of the means for living in a comfortable home.

Teaching conditions include the tools with which one works, the place in which one works, and the amount of work to be done. No one can teach well without an adequate stock of teaching tools. The nature of the tools differs from department to department, but tools there must be. The departments of physical science, of course, require laboratory equipment and material of many sorts. The departments of social science are taking over much of the technique of the physical sciences, and are seeking hungrily for quasi-laboratory facilities, documents, exhibits, and statistical resources with which alone, they say, they can achieve a truly scientific treatment. In the literary fields, the tools are books—many books, more books, and still more books, even beyond the measure of the great book-demands of other fields. Art and music and other subjects have similarly their special needs.

The necessity for the provision of adequate tools is far greater today than it ever was before; for modern teaching in all fields deals more than ever before with the individual, and consists more than ever before in placing the proper tools in his hands, showing him how to use them, telling him to go ahead, standing by to help when help is needed, criticizing the product, and repeating the process, through tasks of graduated difficulty, so long as the instruction lasts.

Only with an adequate stock of modern tools can the teacher teach his best.

Library, laboratory, and classroom must be so planned as to reinforce the teaching process in every possible way. They should all give that fundamental strengthening of morale which comes through abundance of light, through cleanliness, through general pleasantness. And each should be cunningly adapted for its own specific purpose. The laboratory should achieve a triumphant convenience. The books of the modern college library should be made so willingly accessible, and the places where they are read should be places where it is so good to be, as to encourage the formation of a lifelong habit of reading much and reading well.

If the same classroom can be used equally well for political science and for English literature, there is something wrong with the classroom. One of the major influences in my own education was the classroom to which, in my sophomore year, I went for my course in Latin literature. Many another Amherst man will remember it as long as he lives. Its walls were enriched with paintings and large photographs illustrative of classic scenes or classic legends, chosen for no conventional reason but because they somehow possessed a powerful combination of interest, beauty, and interpretative significance. Here and there about the room stood a few small bronzes and marbles—at least they are bronze and marble in my memory. I suppose they were really casts; if so, they were singularly fine in workmanship. They, too, were well chosen. The college boy is more interested in the young Augustus than in the aged Socrates. Here, also, were models of Roman homes and Roman theaters; and in low cases which you passed as you came and went were coins that had been clutched or tossed by Roman hands, *fibulae* that had adorned the garments of Roman merrymakers, cups that had been raised to Roman lips, votive offerings of grateful Roman hearts. Professor Cowles had collected most of these things himself as the years passed. Others had been brought to him by former boys whom he had taught to understand. And how he used the room in his teaching! It was like an orchestra, every element potentially alive, from which, as he would, he drew enrichment for any desired theme.

Only in an adequate environment can the teacher teach his best.

True teaching is hard work. Relentless thoroughness in preparation, mastery of all that is new and should be known, long meditation, wherein the significant and the trivial may reach their true proportions and the essential may stand out in focused clarity—then, in class, the utter eagerness to convey all that which you value so to every one of those whom you value so—and the long drawn-out review of individual reports or experiments . . . . true teaching is hard work—modern teaching, with its individual emphasis, hardest of all.

No man, then, should be given so much of it that the burden will bend him into inefficient weariness. It is obviously poor economy to employ a high-grade man and then so weigh him down that he cannot do the very thing you want him to do. You are not getting that thing done, and you have robbed the world of one good man. The average American college teacher teaches too much. By increase of staff, by limitation of the student body, by the placing of students more and more upon their own responsibility, the energy of the teacher should be so conserved that his every class meeting may be a memorable and a formative event.

Only when the amount of work required is reasonable can the teacher teach his best.

Continued excellence in teaching requires a constant revitalizing of the mind. The very nature of the teaching profession, with its demand that the teacher constantly give forth, indicates the necessity that he should also constantly take in.

This renewal should take place both through reading and through association with other minds. The college, then, should make it possible for the members of its faculty to own and to read the most significant current publications within or related to their several fields; and the college should make it possible for the members of its faculty to mingle with one another in such a way as to produce a mutual enrichment of intellectual resource, and to meet, at local or national gatherings, colleagues engaged in similar work in other institutions.

Only under the enlarging influence of reading and of comradeship can the teacher teach his best.

There are men, and there are great teachers among them, whose creative instinct is satisfied by the teaching process itself, so that they seek no other parallel means of expression. But the very type of mentality which characterizes the good teacher in many cases suggests or even demands that he engage in some parallel form of intellectual creation: it may be direct artistic creation; it may be the interpretation to a wider audience of the significant results of research; it may be research itself.

At this point I should like to bear witness that, in my convinced opinion, there is absolutely no inherent opposition between research and good teaching. I have been clear enough, I hope, in my insistence that for college purposes excellence in teaching is the main thing. I do not regard interest in research as a necessary concomitant of college teaching. And I deplore the wasted energy of men who, under extrinsic pressure, attempt research though they have no gift for it. But if a man has, in addition to teaching ability, the gift of research—if he has really, in the intellectual domain, the adventurous spirit of the pioneer, if he combines wide-ranging imagination and infinite patience—then that gift is to be cultivated as a precious thing: precious not only because of the inherent value of its results, but precious because if rightly utilized in connection with his teaching it may vivify that teaching in the highest degree. The enthusiasm of research tends to permeate all the related teaching field, and the teacher is thus a better teacher because of his research. Moreover, youth loves pioneering. The knowledge of true achievement engenders respect; and if the teacher finds it possible to admit a qualified student to participation, even humble participation, in research, that experience may well become a major factor in the building of the boy's mentality.[1]

Research, then, should be encouraged as a reinforcement of teaching; so should the interpretation of research; so should direct creative writing. The desirability of such activity, from the point of view of its beneficent effect on good teaching, constitutes indeed one of the reasons why the actual teaching load should be kept light.

Only if instinct for research or other creative expression be satisfied can the teacher teach his best.

The efficiency of the teacher is determined

[1] This is the doctrine of President Mason of the University of Chicago, who is seeking, through its application, to give a special stimulus to able undergraduates.

not only by the conditions of his work and by the extent to which his mind is constantly revitalized, but by the conditions of his home life. They indeed, more than anything else, color the lenses through which he sees his students and his work, diminish or enlarge the store of energy whereon he, as teacher, must draw. If the college, then, really desires that a man should teach well, it must make it possible for him to live well. No one proposes, and few desire, luxury; but the men who are to teach our children should be able to live in comfort and in dignity, not untouched with beauty.

The circumstances of professorial life, moreover, react directly upon the student's attitude toward his college work. If the intellectual life of science and of art is seen to reduce its followers to hardship and discontent, its value is thereby discounted in the student's scale. If the professorial home, however simple, is such as to make it a privilege to be welcomed there, the value of all collegiate endeavor rises thereby in student estimate.

Only on the basis of an adequate salary can the teacher teach his best.

Of him to whom much is given, much is to be required. If the college enables a man to teach with adequate tools, in appropriate surroundings, without an excessive instructional burden; if it provides him with opportunities for mental growth and encourages the exercise of his creative energy; and if it makes possible for him a sunny home life—then is that man beholden to serve the college with a deep and grateful loyalty, then is that man in honor bound to teach his best, and to make that best ever better as the years go on.

If the college so selects its teachers and so supports their teaching, and if the teachers so respond to this support, what heights of educational achievement may not be attained?

The ideal teacher, as I have suggested above, is both born and made. It is quite clear that if he isn't born he can't be made. It should be equally clear that his birth conveys no lasting patent of perfection, and that, having been born, he must still be made. To the consideration of his making I now turn.

Believing as we do in the value of our profession, it should be a matter of concern to us that the supply of young men and young women entering it year by year be kept adequate in number and be constantly improved in quality.

The basic condition for the choice of the teaching profession by all those whom we want in it is the attractiveness of the professorial life itself. This matter I have just treated from another point of view. Let me here add simply that an inadequate system of payment not only impairs the teaching efficiency of those who are underpaid, but tends to turn away from the teaching profession discerning students who might otherwise enter it.

But the attractiveness of an ideal professorial life is not necessarily enough to win a boy to teaching. The ablest men, as they near graduation, are nowadays more and more likely to be sought out by representatives of business houses or other organizations who offer substantial inducements for enlistment. Is there any reason why the teaching profession itself should not so recruit? If a professor comes to believe that one of his students would make a particularly good teacher, should he not, as a matter of professional loyalty, seek to bring him into the profession? In many cases a frank talk on this problem between professor and student should be possible. If relations between professor and student are not so simple as to prevent embarrassment, the dean or the president might perhaps with greater freedom set the matter forth.

If now a student, while still an undergraduate, has decided to teach, how shall he be trained for his chosen work? The answer is in theory perfectly simple. In addition to mastering the content of his special subject through courses and other work in the department concerned, he should learn something of the methods and aims of education as such through courses and other work in the department of education. Such practical difficulties as exist in the application of this theory are due primarily to the mutual distrust of departments of education and other departments—a distrust which forms a sorry chapter in our recent educational history. Neither party is without fault, nor is either party wholly wrong. Various causes are now operating to reduce that mutual distrust. May it soon diminish into insignificance!

Take now the case of the graduate student who, in the hope of preparing himself for a college position, enters a graduate school. Here again the theory would seem to be clear. He enters that graduate school as a vocational school, in order that he may qualify himself to earn a livelihood in a position in which his primary duty is to be teaching. Clearly, then, his graduate experience should include study of the teaching of his chosen subject, and of the general enterprise of higher education.

This problem differs in two respects from the problem of undergraduate training in education. In the first place, graduate departments of education are equipped primarily to give instruction regarding secondary education, and are not as a rule prepared to give instruction regarding college education. In the second place, teaching in college, while it is closely akin to secondary teaching, is necessarily more specialized in content and in method. It would, then, perhaps be most appropriate that each graduate department should maintain its own courses for the training of its students as teachers, and that the department of education should maintain a limited number of generalized courses in teaching and in the field of higher education as a whole. Perhaps some such distribution of the task as this may serve to establish a better co-operation between graduate departments of education and other departments.

Graduate training at the present time suffers from overemphasis on research. I have already indicated my high esteem for research, both in itself and as a reinforcement of teaching; and I speak from an experience in which research has played a large and happy part. My belief in the value of research is indeed so strong that I should heartily assent to the proposition that any student preparing himself for college teaching should be tried out in the field of research, so that whatever gift he has for it may be fully developed. But I do suggest, in this regard, a shift in emphasis: a lessening of the emphasis on research as an all but exclusive means and sign of qualification for a teaching position, and a corresponding increase in the amount of direct graduate training for teaching as such.

Such a change in emphasis would be much facilitated if college officers, in their dealings with the heads of graduate departments with regard to candidates, would insist on the production of evidence as to teaching ability; and if college presidents, after a year's employment of a university-trained appointee, would report to the officers of the graduate school in which he received his training the facts as to his good or ill success in the year's work.

In no case is it fair to assume that an instructor who fails to make good fails exclusively because of faulty training in the graduate school. The cause of failure may well lie farther back, or be inherent. But the graduate school, if it consents, as it may well do, to extend its opportunities to certain students who give no indication of the possession or the development of teaching ability, should at least play fair with such students by telling them that it cannot recommend them as teachers, and with college officers by refusing unjustified recommendations.

The training of the young teacher does not, or should not, end in the graduate school. It should continue into the early years of his collegiate service. Just as the young medical student, after the completion of his course of study, spends a year or more in internship, practicing under the guidance and with the support of experienced men, so the instructor, as he enters upon his life-work, should for his own sake and for the sake of his students, present and future, receive still further training from some member of the staff of the department which he has entered.

Such training should proceed primarily through report and conference. The instructor, that is, should bring to his adviser from time to time reports, formal or informal, of work done, of experiments tried, of results achieved, of difficulties solved or unsolved; and he should bring as well, in these modern days, individual data as to the qualifications, progress, and difficulties of the several students in his course or courses. The adviser, then, after careful study of the material thus submitted, should make constructive suggestions as to the instructor's further work. Classroom visitation by the adviser is not a necessary part of the training scheme. It may prove desirable, but if so it should come after adviser and instructor are well acquainted, and it should come as a means, mutually desired, for the observation of a particular experiment or the solution of a particular difficulty.

This is but the merest sketch of possibilities which would be worked out very differently under differing circumstances. The essential thing is that there should be established, between the older members of the department and the newcomer, a relationship designed, in the friendliest spirit, to help the newcomer to find and to develop himself in his actual service as teacher.

And when the period of such advisory training ceases, there should ensue a period of self-training which should last—as indeed I have suggested above—throughout the rest of the man's career. No man's teaching is ever so good as to leave no room for improvement. No man's teaching is ever so good as to justify the deterioration which is the inevitable alternative of development.

The main factors in this lifelong self-training are three: experimentation, reading, and comparing notes with colleagues. If the same material be presented by different methods in different courses, whether in the same year or different years, the instructor should be able to draw a sound inference as to which method is better, and should thereafter adopt that method in preference to the other. The habit of experimentation is, furthermore, a good thing in itself, for it serves continually to sharpen a man's interest in the artistry of his own teaching. Much is written nowadays on the subject of college teaching which is just as well worth the attention of the college teacher as are the current publications in the subject matter of his own field. And the teacher has no more right to neglect the bibliography of the teaching profession than a scholar to neglect the bibliography of his own field of research. The comparison of notes with colleagues may be purely casual or informal, or may take the form of conference or discussion.

I turn next and finally to a very general treatment of the question of method in college teaching.

Current methods are necessarily of two main types: classroom methods and the laboratory method. The latter, originating in and primarily appropriate to the physical sciences, needs little or no discussion. Its strength lies in its individualism and in its combination of the mastery of fact with the use of fact. Its potential weakness lies in the danger that it may degenerate into a mere following of directions without a full appreciation of the significance of process or result.

The two traditional classroom methods are the lecture and the recitation. The ultimate reason why we have a lecture method is because universities were founded before the invention of printing. The teaching profession, despite five centuries of printing, has not yet shaken off the medieval attitude; the teacher has not yet fully realized that many books on his subject, good books, books written possibly by even greater men than he, are readily accessible to his students. The presentation through lecture of large blocks of material which are in substance readily available in print is inexcusable. Furthermore, the lecture process as a means of conveying information simply doesn't work with the typical modern undergraduate. If there be anyone who doubts this statement, let him read Professor Richardson's delightful and not overdrawn discussion of student note-taking,[1] and let him supplement it with honest memories of notebooks which he has himself beheld.

I do not, of course, mean to imply that all lecturing is bad. There are many cases in which it is necessary and desirable. It is the normal

[1] L. B. Richardson, *A Study of the Liberal College* (A Report to the President of Dartmouth College), Hanover, 1924, pp. 195–97.

means for the communication of knowledge not yet available in print, or for significant new interpretation of knowledge already so available. It is the normal means for the conveyance of directions or unifying suggestions specific to a given course. It may provide demonstration or illustration not otherwise possible. In the case of a large institution, the occasional or periodic lecture by a department head in an elementary course may be a unique and invaluable means of bringing the student into contact with a mature creative mind. The lecture does indeed always carry—for better or worse—a sense of personality which the printed page rarely achieves. But the lecture is always to be used with full consciousness of its limitations and its dangers.

The recitation method, like the lecture method, has the advantage of being, for the teacher, very easy. In its purest and simplest form it is a means of finding out, by oral sampling in the presence of the whole class, whether certain individual members of the class have learned what they have been told to learn. It is a method of testing rather than of teaching—and a wasteful method at that.

But the recitation method hardly exists in the modern college in its pure and simple form, except perhaps in certain elementary courses which ought not to be in college at all.

It is passing over gradually into the method of discussion—a "modern" method employed with memorable success by Socrates, and by great teachers of every succeeding age. It is indissolubly associated with care for the individual learner, and with a willingness on the part of the teacher to spend himself in his teaching. For it is as hard as the other methods are easy. It involves the preparation of material for discussion—the selection of such available treatments of the subject as will most naturally stir student interest. It involves a differentiation in the assignment of this material; for the clash of minds is far more likely to come if different students have read books or articles expressing different viewpoints. It involves in the classroom an alert, imaginative sense of what is going on in each brain, a sympathetic understanding of difficulties, a sporting delight in bringing significance out of insignificance. It involves a willingness, a resolution, even, to play the smallest possible part one's self, to serve rather as a fair presiding officer than as judge or jury, to get young Royce to answer the question young James has asked. It is likely to involve the tactful suppression of some student whose thoughts dwell on the tip of an active tongue; and it is sure to involve the quiet enlistment from time to time of those who from shyness—and there are many such—would prefer to sit and listen.

Such teaching is hard beyond the ordinary measure of hardness, but it brings rich and immediate and permanent reward, both in its certainty of specific result and in the abiding knowledge that it has contributed to the fashioning and the strengthening of men's minds.

The note of individualism has been struck more than once in the foregoing paragraphs. The appreciation of the value of the individual personality and the recognition of individual differences—doctrines which, again, are as old as our era, and older—have come in the last decade to mark specifically our progressive educational effort. We have tried mass production in the educational field, and have found it dismally wanting. The personnel lessons of the war have proved readily transferable to the problems of peace. Psychological advance has pointed in the same direction—and so has the eternal spirit of the true teacher.

We are making more and more extensive use of the principle of the student's individual responsibility, daring to build again on the great Aristotelian premise: "All men have by nature the desire to know."

This spirit underlies the recent movement toward the substitution of individual study in the later years of the college course for part of the ordinarily required course-taking. Allied with it is the belief that the mere taking of courses seldom leads to real mastery of a subject, and that there should be in the field of major interest some means of covering the portions of the field not covered in courses, and of synthesizing all work done in the field, whether in or out of course. On this spirit and belief is built the plan of major work now in effect at Harvard, Princeton, and elsewhere, which has as its outer sign and gateway the general final examination in the major study, and is supported by some measure of tutorial or preceptorial guidance.

Akin to this movement, on the side of individualism, are the proposals made in the preceding chapter with regard to self-initiation into some one new field and with regard to general reading.

The recognition of individual differences compels the recognition of differences in ability. Even with the process of selective admission, the college still receives students who range in intellectual caliber from excellence to inferiority. And we are realizing more and more that we cannot rightly apply the same educational treatment to students of several different grades. In particular we are realizing that, as trustees for society, we should devote all possible special care to the development of the ablest students.

This principle and the two main modern forms of its application—the sectioning of students on the basis of ability and the honors course—have been treated in a preceding essay.[1]

The coming years will bring new experiments, new methods. The endeavor to create

[1] See above, pp. 7–11.

in this line is indeed as worthy—and as hard—as any other task of imagination or of research. Improvement comes slowly; the inertia of long and easy habit resists invasion. Much that we have achieved is definitely good and may well be permanent. Yet there is, and there will always be, need for reappraisal and for fresh approach.

IV

WHO SHALL GO TO COLLEGE?

The question as stated is a composite of four questions asked by the four different persons immediately concerned: the boy or girl, the family, the school, and the college.

For the boy or girl the question is: "Shall I go to college?" And the eager mind, alert with the "desire to know," kindled with idealism, craving excitement, pressed on by a sense of social conformity, tends naturally to answer "Yes."

For the family the question is: "Shall we send John—or Mary—to college?" Against a background shadowy with the reluctant thought of separation, the debate ranges through the fields of experience and report, conditioned by circumstances, pressed on, again, by a sense of social conformity, alive, again, with a vicarious desire to know and to serve, swaying between proud hope and fears vague or definite.

For the school, in turn, the question is: "Whom shall we recommend for college entrance?"—a searching question, which must be answered with justice alike toward pupil, toward family, and toward college.

For the college, faced with a welcome and

yet menacing flood of applicants, the question becomes: "Whom shall we admit?" Here, too, conflict precedes decision; for the college, like any other person, rejoices in growth and, believing in itself, hesitates to deny its treasure to those who seek. Yet the college has not the resources to take care of all; and it is forever learning that the desire to enter is no proof of fitness. Nor can the college choose on the arbitrary basis of its own immediate liking.

For the final answer to the fourfold question will be given not by the boy or girl, not by the family, not by the school, not by the college, but by that human society within which the individual and the family live and move and exchange sustenance, the society which supports the school as an indispensable means to its own future self-control, the society which in the last analysis supports the college in the hope of receiving therefrom the leaders it so greatly needs for the solution of its devastating problems, for the realization of its untold and wondrous opportunities. On the lips of this composite person, way-worn, resolute, and ever young with hope, the question becomes at last: "Who shall go to college?"

The answer, inevitably, and quite simply, is this: "Every potential leader—and no one else."

Let me make clear at once two points with regard to this definition. In the first place, I am using the word "leader" as synonymous with

WHO SHALL GO TO COLLEGE?

the phrase "true leader"—to mean, that is, "a leader who will use his leadership for the good of society." In the second place, the leadership contemplated does not necessarily imply public prominence. It embraces leadership of the first order, which involves vision and endeavor of outstanding significance, and leadership of the second order, which involves vision and endeavor of smaller range, together with that intelligent support of leaders of the first order without which even their leadership cannot achieve its full success.

Every potential leader, then, and no one else, should go to college. The family and the school have no social right *not* to send to college every boy or girl who gives promise of true leadership; and they have no right to send anyone else. The college has no social right not to welcome, up to the limits of its capacity, all applicants who give promise of true leadership; and it has no right to admit anyone else. For college, school, and family alike hold the precious individual, through childhood and through youth, in trust for society; and society cannot afford that anyone who might become a leader should miss the fullest training for leadership, or that the training of its potential leaders should be impaired by the dissonant presence of the hostile or the unqualified.

What, then, are the signs of potential leadership; and how, at the time of college entrance, shall they be ascertained and rated?

There is no inevitable list of the qualities indicative of leadership. I am content to accept as a working basis a list composed co-operatively by a number of University of Chicago teachers and students. It contains twenty qualities. The first nine, primarily intellectual, are:

1. Technical ability (workmanship, dexterity)
2. Power of expression
3. Accuracy of observation
4. Perseverance
5. Power of concentration
6. Sense of proportion (including a sense of humor)
7. Intellectual curiosity
8. Power of initiative
9. Ability to reason, comprising
    a) Possession of facts
    b) Analysis of facts
    c) Synthesis of facts
    d) Interpretation of facts

Such qualities are the essential stuff of which leadership is made. The development of these qualities is the central concern of the college.

The next four qualities, primarily physical, are:

10. Health of body
11. Appearance
12. Manner (bearing)
13. Attractiveness (charm)

Such qualities are the support and the reinforcement of leadership. Without health and without magnetism leadership is certain to falter and is likely to fail. Nor are these magic gifts; they may be won and cultivated through intelligence, resolution, and welcomed guidance.

The last seven qualities, primarily moral, are:

14. Ability to co-operate
15. Moral cleanness
16. Honesty
17. Faith in knowledge
18. Purposefulness
19. Vision
20. Social-mindedness

Such qualities give to leadership its motive force and its directive control. Without them a man or woman richly possessed of the preceding qualities might remain in selfish aloofness, or, worse yet, might use his or her powers for anti-social ends—might be no leader, but a slacker or a traitor to society.

Such then are the qualities indicative of leadership. What measure of possession of such qualities serves at the age of college entrance to indicate potential leadership? The term "possession" as so used must, of course, include not only actual possession but definite promise of development.

We cannot ask for the possession of all the foregoing qualities in a high degree. We cannot accept the possession of but a few; nor the possession of many held in only average degree. Nor can we predicate leadership of a student markedly lacking in any one of the three groups of qualities. I should, therefore, define the potential leader as one who possesses, or gives definite promise of developing, many of these qualities in notable degree. He, or she, then, should go to college.

How, now, shall it be determined whether a student does in fact possess or give promise of developing such qualities in a measure adequate for college demand and opportunity?

The initiative lies, of course, with the individual and the family. If they believe that the student does adequately possess such qualities, and if the school seconds the belief, the question then comes for final decision to the college; which, being alone responsible for its standards, must be the sole final judge.

The first step on the part of the college should be the inspection of the student's high-school record. This inspection should give weight primarily to intellectual achievement, since the capacity for such achievement is the most direct indication of the possession of the essential stuff of leadership, and since intellectual achievement may be measured more objectively than most of the other qualities concerned. But even this inspection should take into account all other data available in written form with regard to the student.

If the inspection leaves the applicant as still a possible candidate, the next step should be, ideally, a special conference, in every case, of the four persons concerned: the student, the family, the school, the college. Such a conference would have two main purposes: it would enable the college to ascertain as well as possible the student's degree of promise in respects not adequately covered by the written record; and it would enable the student and the family to gain information as to conditions of life and work at the college additional to and more personal than the information contained in the official documents of the college. I use the word "conference" advisedly, rather than the word "interview"; for the study I have in mind is more extensive and more searching than anything which the word "interview" can properly denote. The conference might take place either at the college or elsewhere. In many cases, particularly in the case of a country college, there would be obvious advantages in economy of time if the college representative should maintain an office temporarily in a city or town in which several applicants live.

The inspection of the high-school record and the conference should be supplemented, whenever the college remains in the least doubt, by a limited number of carefully devised examinations.

If the college is to undertake such a program as this it must devote to its admissions work, personal and documentary, the full time of a highly competent director of admissions, with such assistants as he or she may need. The ideal is high, but it is by no means unpracticable. It is indeed already being more and more nearly approached by some of the more progressive colleges.

Only the realization of such a plan will put an end to the tragic errors that now mark so frequently the process of college entrance. Only so will there be an end to the student's facing conditions of life and work of which neither he nor his family has had adequate information. Only so will there be an end to the exclusion of students whose real promise of leadership is obscured by the conventional documents. Only so will there be an end to the admission of students foredoomed to the life-long disappointment of an academic failure which they might have been spared. Only so can the possibility of physical or mental or moral breakdown be reduced to the vanishing point. Only so can the college guard itself and society against the training of those who are not likely to use their developed powers for the common good.

If the college decides not to admit the applicant, the reasoned statement of that decision would be the greatest kindness the college could render him. The statement should indicate whether the decision is permanent or temporary —that is, whether it might or might not be reversed in case the student should later develop qualities not then evident. It should if possible indicate constructively an occupation appropriate for the student. An adverse decision would

WHO SHALL GO TO COLLEGE?

naturally bring disappointment, but it is far better that such disappointment should come then rather than at the end of a year wasted or worse than wasted.

The entire problem of admission can best be handled, in all respects, by a college which has definitely limited the number of students it will receive.

I have not spoken hitherto of the problem of cost. From the social point of view, every potential leader should go to college, regardless of the cost. It is, then, the duty of society to make college education possible for every potential leader. The state universities are meeting this obligation in one perfectly logical way —through taxation. The privately endowed colleges are in general meeting the need in a traditional way which, however appropriate a hundred years ago when colleges were few and were largely engaged in the preparation of candidates for the ministry, is no less than absurd as extended in our day and generation to a nation-wide collegiate system. For the colleges are in general charging each student about half of what his or her education actually costs— that is, they are giving a half-scholarship to every student whether he needs it or not—and they are furthermore giving complete scholarships to a considerable number of those who do need them. I cannot believe that the colleges will be content to continue much longer on so obviously unsound a financial basis. Rather should they charge each student the full amount of the actual cost of his education, and then, fortified by the increased income thus available, make liberal adjustments in the case of desirable students who cannot meet the charge in full or cannot meet it at all. In such cases a long-term loan, running perhaps without interest for ten years after graduation, would in general be a better device than an outright scholarship.

For the present the problem of cost must be met in whatever way may be possible— through selection of a tax-supported college, through scholarships, through private borrowing, through continued or intermittent earning by the student. But in any case the potential leader should go to college if the expense can be met by any sacrifice less costly than the loss of his or her potential leadership.

So, too, the potential leader should go to college despite the fact that the college is a very imperfect institution. In no respect is it all that it ought to be. It does not give adequate care to the maintenance and development of individual health. It does not make adequate provision for wise guidance in the many social, moral, and religious problems that crowd the years of modern adolescence. Its methods of instruction are not yet fully individualized. The life of its faculty members still lacks the serene dignity which, for the sake of society, should be the portion of those who hold so high a trust.

WHO SHALL GO TO COLLEGE? 83

But in these and in other respects the college is striving for improvement and is making notable progress. And the college, with all its imperfections, is our only great instrument for the development of potential leadership.

If your children are potential leaders, send them then, despite misgivings. Send them strong in body, established to the utmost of your ability in the habits of health. Send them strong in mind, ready for the great adventure of learning, resolute to achieve, reverent of truth. Send them strong in spirit, loving, eager to serve, loyal to the human bond. Send them gladly withal, in reasoned hope, in surging confidence.

Send them, but come with them too. You *will* come with them, inevitably, in so far as you have entered into and molded their lives. But we need more than that. We need your constant knowledge of our general purposes and problems; and we need your constant reinforcement in the specific endeavor to bring to its full development the potential leadership of your son or of your daughter.

And we on our part will do our utmost to make the college worthy of those who send, and of those who come.

V

AN INCIDENT IN FRESHMAN REGISTRATION

The process of selective admission, as now generally administered, assembles an immense amount of information about the individual applicant—records and letters from high-school officials and teachers, letters from other men and women who have known him, answers by the applicant himself to a long series of varied questions, and, in many cases, an autobiography.

The immediate function of this material is to enable the college to determine whether or not the student should be admitted. But the material is far too valuable to be discarded after the fulfilment of that first purpose. It is the normal basis for that individual consideration of the student which we now seek to give, in increasing measure, throughout his college course.

When a boy finally comes to college, the first officer of the college to whom he actually talks is the dean or adviser to whom he goes for registration. The importance of this first contact can hardly be overestimated. If it is hurried and mechanical, it sets in the mind of the bewildered student the impression that the col-

AN INCIDENT

lege is a huge and relentless machine. If, on the other hand, it is wise, friendly, and individualized, the student enters with a far more eager spirit upon his new path.

Obviously, then, the deans or advisers who are to have the responsibility of this first contact should prepare themselves for it by studying the individualized admission material—each studying, of course, the papers of the particular students whom he is to register. If this is rightly done, the dean will be able, as each student comes before him, to greet him with some friendly knowledge of his individual experience and interests.

An incident which befell me in this connection so clearly illustrates the possibilities just suggested, and is so deeply and happily imprinted in my memory, that I venture to put it on record here.

The plan of the utilization of admission papers by the registering deans went into effect in the University of Chicago in September, 1923. Shortly before the first day of registration the ten deans who were to register freshmen were gathered in my office for conference as to methods of procedure. Each had before him the pile of admission papers—about seventy-five in each pile—of the freshmen whom he was to register.

As my work at registration was to be merely supervisory, I had no such pile of papers before me. But as the conference proceeded, desiring to put myself intelligently into the position of a registering dean, I pulled out a paper, purely at random, from the pile nearest me, and read it.

It was a very creditable paper, though it did not at first strike me as exceptionally notable. The boy had read more widely than usual, and had read things worth reading. He had listed debating as his special hobby; and in answer to the question: "Of all the things you have accomplished, which have given you the greatest satisfaction?" he had replied: "Being a member of my high-school debating team, and being elected president of my class Senior year." Then followed the autobiography, which again was highly creditable, but not striking—until the last sentence was reached. That last sentence was this: "I have been unable to fill out this blank in my own handwriting as requested, because I am blind."

I re-read the paper—and with admiration.

On registration day, in the great hall used for the purpose, the ten registering deans sat at their desks, and the freshmen assigned to each dean reported to him for registration and for information.

My station, as supervisor, was on the platform. Just one of the seven hundred and fifty freshmen, instead of going to his dean, was brought straight to me. It was the very boy whose paper I had chanced to read!

How much the personal character of my greeting meant to him I do not know. To me

AN INCIDENT

that interview is memorable, both because I was proud then and am proud now to know that boy, and because the coincidence exemplified for me with such extraordinary emphasis the possibility of individualization in the reception of incoming freshmen.

VI

FRESHMAN WEEK

When one is entering on a new phase of experience, it is, of course, extremely important to get started right, for the impressions received and the tendencies which appear at the outset are likely to harden into opinions and habits which may be of momentous weight in determining the course of the life that is to follow.

Entrance into college affords a crisis of just this type. The first term is likely to govern later terms, and the first week of the first term is likely to imprint its character on the later weeks. So much is new—an environment new not only in that it is locally different but in that it is not home; associates, older and contemporary, almost completely new; a type of teaching and a type of study new in scope and in intensity; an endless variety of new and miscellaneous interests—so much is new that it is no wonder that many a freshman has grown bewildered and discouraged and has fallen into habits and associations that tend to counteract the educational purpose rather than to reinforce it.

Clearly, then, if a college is interested in the success and welfare of its newcomers, it is worth while to concentrate for a few days on

FRESHMAN WEEK

the task of adjusting freshmen rightly to their new situation. This idea is not novel; but it has recently been developed on a much larger scale than previously. "Freshman Week" was first instituted in 1923, by the University of Maine.

The University of Chicago tried the experiment a year later. The present paper is a record of that experiment.

Our special major purposes were four: to complete before the opening of college all matters connected with the routine of entrance and registration for courses; to give the freshmen sound advice on the major problems of college life and specific advice and direction as to many immediate problems and requirements; to give them a chance to get settled and to get acquainted with the University as a whole; and to give them a genuine welcome into the college community. Being firm believers in the practice of faculty-student co-operation, we asked various student organizations to help us in formulating and carrying out our plans, and we enjoyed their cordial and indispensable assistance.

During the summer each freshman received a course book (our general official handbook) and an eight-page leaflet of "Instructions and Suggestions for First-Year College Students," containing certain general information, a full program of Freshman Week, and a list of all of the courses ordinarily open to freshmen, with brief information about each course. The course books were stamped with numbers corresponding to the order in which the freshmen had applied for entrance.

We called the freshmen together on Thursday, September 25, six days before college opened. For the first four days of the period, the freshman women not living at home were housed without charge in one of the University halls. The University Commons, the men's club, and our social hall for women were kept open throughout the period.

The entire class met for the first time early on Thursday morning. The University marshals—senior students of high standing—in cap and gown, served on this and other occasions to insure prompt and orderly entrance and seating. A brief address of welcome was made by the President of the University, who spoke of the University's concern for scholarship, for consideration for the individual, for social-mindedness, for character, and for religion. The President of the Undergraduate Student Council added a word of welcome from the student body; and the Dean of the Colleges of Arts, Literature, and Science explained the program for the week and gave general directions and suggestions for the use of the time not taken up by the stated engagements.

The rest of Thursday morning, all of Thursday afternoon, and all of Friday morning were devoted to registration. Students with course books numbered from 1 to 250—that is, the first 250 students who had applied for entrance —had been told to register on Thursday morning; those with course books numbered from 251 to 500, on Thursday afternoon; those with course books numbered from 501 up, on Friday morning. This division, together with a subsidiary system of specific registration appointments and the presence of ten registering deans, made registration an orderly process and prevented, in theory and to a large extent in practice, unnecessary waiting on the part of the freshmen.

To each dean a particular group of freshmen had been assigned; and each dean, before registration, had read the entrance papers of each freshman assigned to him, and was able, therefore, to greet each newcomer with some knowledge of his individual experience and some familiarity with his specific interests and needs. The registration process was made a real interview, not a mechanical signing of cards. Incidentally, each dean had prepared a list of a few selected students of superior ability who were to be invited to enter the special freshman cooperative course on "The Nature of the World and of Man."

Immediately after registration, each student went to the men's or the women's gymnasium to take a physical examination or to make an appointment for such an examination. Thanks to the enlistment of a sufficient staff of doctors, almost the entire series of physical examinations was finished before the opening of college.

All students were advised to pay their fees and buy their books as soon as possible after registration, and many of them did so, thus lessening greatly the usual congestion at the opening of the term.

On Thursday evening the first social entertainments were given, one for the men, organized by the Y.M.C.A., and one for the women, organized by the Women's Athletic Association.

On Friday afternoon the class met again as a body to hear the first of four "Talks to Freshmen," at which attendance was required. The first talk, by the Dean of the Colleges, dealt with the purpose of a college education and the responsibility of the newcomers to prepare themselves for leadership, suggested a general proportion of values for the main college interests—5 for study, 2 for social relations of all sorts, 1 for athletics, and 1 for activities; and dealt, finally, with the principles which should govern the choice of a fraternity and with the particular problems of the opening days. After the meeting, copies of a specially planned issue of the college daily, the *Maroon*, were distributed free to all members of the class.

Immediately after this meeting came the first of three English tests, required of all freshmen, for the purpose of determining whether they should be exempted from the

English course ordinarily required of students in the first term, or required to take it, or excluded from it because of a particularly low grade; and, if required to take it, whether they should be assigned to a high, a medium, or a low section—in accordance with the principle of sectioning on the basis of ability.

Late in the afternoon a special meeting of all women expecting to live in the University halls was addressed by the Dean of Women.

On Friday evening the University gave a reception to the members of the incoming class and to their parents, and was particularly glad to welcome many parents at this time. Membes of the Federation of University Women acted informally as hostesses on this occasion.

On Saturday and Sunday no required appointments were scheduled, except individual appointments for physical examinations.

On Saturday morning voluntary sight-seeing tours of the University were conducted by the Y.M.C.A. and the Federation of University Women. Each group, in the course of its tour, spent a half-hour in the University Library and was there instructed in the use of the Library by a member of the Library staff.

In the afternoon a practice football game was played, both teams being drawn from the University football squad. The game was followed by a dance, arranged by the sophomore societies, Skull and Crescent and Sign of the Sickle, and given in the men's club.

On Sunday afternoon a vesper service was held, to which the parents of the freshmen as well as the freshmen themselves were invited. The address was made by the President of the University, who spoke of the place of religion in college life, of the experience of change in religious belief which is normally characteristic of college life, and of the rightness of combining firm hold on that which is essential with readiness to enlarge and broaden religious thought and experience in the light of the new enrichment of life that college should bring.

On Sunday evening a musicale was given under the direction of the Undergraduate Student Council.

Monday morning was occupied with the second and third official talks and with the second English test. The first of the two talks, by the health officer of the University, dealt in practical detail with the care and preservation of health; the second, by the University cashier, with the care of money, particular stress being laid on the wisdom of preparing and living by a budget and on the importance of promptness and reliability in all financial matters.

In the afternoon, sight-seeing tours were again conducted, and the freshman women were given the use of the swimming tank in the women's gymnasium. In the evening a party for the freshman women was given by the Y.W.C.A.

On Tuesday morning the Director of the

School of Education gave the last of the talks, on "How to Study." He contrasted inefficient and efficient methods of work and dwelt in particular on the right way of reading—the resolute survey of an assignment as a whole prior to the detailed study of a particular part of it—and on free reading—that is, the habit of consulting books other than the textbook—as preferable to enslaved dependence on a single text.

Later in the morning the third and last of the English tests was given. In the afternoon the entire class took the Thurstone psychological tests; afterward the Dean of Women and some other speakers, teachers and students, addressed a meeting of the freshman women, for whom a tea was then given by the University.

Throughout the period the fraternities carried on their rushing, and by Tuesday the pledging process was very nearly complete. Thus, when college work actually began, on Wednesday, October 1, the freshmen were duly matriculated, soundly advised, well settled, cordially welcomed, and, in general, ready for real work.

The experiment served to convince us fully of the value of Freshman Week, and it has become a part of the regular autumn procedure. Each year brings its own variations and improvements in the details of the program.

VII

FACULTY-STUDENT CO-OPERATION

The persons who know most at any one time about the actual conditions of college life and work are the students themselves—particularly, of course, the upperclassmen. They not only know conditions, but they feel about them and think about them. The traditional lines of least resistance for both thought and feeling are in the direction of negative discontent rather than of reflective suggestion. Yet the average intelligence of the typical college body is in reality high, and the intelligence of its ablest members is very high indeed; the typical college body is inherently idealistic, and its ablest members in particular are quickly responsive to a reasoned appeal for constructive service. It would seem to be the part of wisdom, therefore, that any administration seeking to improve the conditions of college life and work should utilize to the full the great potential energy of student thought and idealism.

This does not mean that students should be set to work alone in vital matters—for they have not the maturity of judgment, nor the fund of educational knowledge and experience, nor the training in investigative and legislative

FACULTY AND STUDENTS

procedure which would render probable the attainment of adequate and tenable results. Nor should the administration and faculty work alone—since to do so would be to disregard first-hand knowledge and readily available working power.

The improvement of the conditions of college life and work should therefore be, to a far larger extent than is at present the case, a matter of faculty-student co-operation.

I shall endeavor in what follows to give first a brief account of recent experience in faculty-student co-operation at the University of Chicago, and then to add thereto some further suggestions as to the principles and values of such co-operation.

I

In the autumn of 1923 there arose a problem regarding an organization of undergraduate men in the University of Chicago which, while of no great significance in itself, was critical as being likely to determine the attitude of the student body toward a then new administration. It was in this instance perfectly clear that student opinion should be fully heard and duly weighed. There was therefore appointed a committee consisting, in addition to the chairman, of four members of the faculty and four leading men of the senior class. At the first meeting of this committee the faculty members sat on one side of a long table and the students sat on the other side. The students were at first reticent and the faculty members a little uncertain as to means and values of discussion. But in the course of the evening it became evident to the faculty members that the students had the basic knowledge and the will to work and were as good companions in thought as could be desired; and it became evident to the students that the faculty members were not trying to "put anything over," but sincerely wanted facts and suggestions and were not averse to having their own ideas criticized or refuted. In the later sessions of the committee there was no separation of faculty from students in seating or in mental attitude. The committee produced what was generally regarded as a sound and wise report; but the main value of its work was the proof that faculty and students could work together gladly and effectively in a matter of mutual concern.

The success of this committee and the increasing disposition of students, in part resulting therefrom, to bring to administrative attention matters which in student opinion needed consideration led in the winter of 1923–24 to the organization of a co-operative movement known as the "Better Yet Campaign."

This movement was itself in charge of an executive committee on which faculty and students were equally represented. All members of the senior class were invited to participate in the campaign by sending in written suggestions as to conditions in the field of student life and work which might well be studied with a view to improvement. The many suggestions received were canvassed by the executive committee, and twenty-two were selected for study. The topics thus chosen were—in addition to some of purely local and temporary interest—the following: the establishment of a department or school of music; the providing of more courses in public speaking; the development of interest in current affairs; the distribution of students' time; the improvement of the quality of instruction in elementary courses; the introduction of an activity point system; the direction of student activities; the establishment of a freshman men's club; student representation on the Board of Student Organizations; the composition and activities of the Honor Commission; the development of class spirit; faculty fraternity counselors; a club or clubs for non-fraternity men; a club or clubs for non-club women; undergraduate religious life; the supervision of social functions; the student auditor plan; intramural athletics.

For each of these topics the executive committee appointed a special faculty-student committee, the question of personnel being studied with great care. The typical committee consisted of a faculty chairman, three other faculty members, and three students, chiefly but not exclusively seniors. Duplication in the membership of these committees was avoided; consequently a high percentage of the leading upperclassmen were enlisted in the movement.

Some of these committees finished their work before the end of the winter. Others continued in service for more than a year. In nearly every case definite results were reached and recommendations embodied in the committee report have been carried into effect. The report of the Committee on the Distribution of Students' Time, a very notable piece of educational research, has been printed and has been found valuable not only at Chicago but elsewhere. A portion of the report of the Committee on the Quality of Instruction in Elementary Courses has been printed under the title "Qualities Desirable in Instructors in Elementary Courses Conducted by the Lecture-Discussion Method."[1]

But the most significant results of the movement as a whole were the experience of co-operation itself, the educational training afforded to students through the prosecution of informal study in companionship with faculty members, and the renewed proof that faculty and students could thus work together with mutual pleasure and to real advantage.

In two cases reports of "Better Yet" committees led to the establishment of a permanent faculty-student body. The official University Board of Student Organizations, Publications, and Exhibitions, which has general control of

[1] See above, p. 50, n. 1.

fraternities, clubs, student activities, and social affairs, had consisted hitherto of about a dozen faculty members without student representation. The Better Yet Committee in question recommended that from two to four students be added to the Board as regular members. This recommendation was accepted by the Board itself, by the University Senate, and by the Board of Trustees (as it involved a change in the statutes of the University); and since the spring of 1924 the Board of Student Organizations has had the very great advantage of having students in its membership. Student opinion is thus adequately represented, and students know that the matters concerned have been fully and freely and considerately discussed. The student members of the Board are regular members in every respect, and share with the faculty members in the committee work of the Board.

The Honor Commission at Chicago is the body which tries cases of students accused of dishonesty in written work or in examination, and awards penalties in cases of guilt. For some time prior to the Better Yet Campaign the Honor Commission had been composed exclusively of students. The results were very unsatisfactory. Elections to the commission were to a large extent political; there was not and could not well be a real consistency or continuity in policy; and the Commission failed to retain the confidence of either the faculty or the student body. The Honor Commission as reconstituted on recommendation of the Better Yet Committee is now a joint faculty-student body with a faculty chairman. It has already demonstrated its great superiority over the earlier form.

Other faculty-student committees have come into existence as a consequence of the development—again the work of a Better Yet Committee—of the faculty fraternity counselor plan. Each fraternity has a faculty counselor; these counselors are organized as a body with committees on various subjects; and each such committee asks the Undergraduate Interfraternity Council to appoint a committee of students to work with it. One such joint committee, for instance, has been very helpful with a plan related to the raising of fraternity scholarship; and another in the drafting of a standard set of fraternity-house rules.

The principle of co-operation thus amply established as valid has found and is finding other less formal expressions. Prior to 1924 the Dean of the Colleges handled singly or with special faculty advice such disciplinary cases as did not fall within the field of the Honor Commission. In the autumn of 1924 the Dean asked the Undergraduate Council to appoint a committee of four undergraduates to sit as advisers to the Dean in such disciplinary cases. The Dean retains the right of decision; but the questioning and the expressions of opinion of the students have been exceedingly valuable. This plan has made for justice and for the general knowledge that justice is sincerely sought and measurably obtained.

It has become the practice of the Dean, when some move affecting the conditions of student life and work has been contemplated, to call in a group of upperclassmen for informal discussion of the plan while it is still tentative and fluid. So, for instance, the policy by which a fraternity is placed on probation (i.e., is forbidden to initiate or to hold social functions) for a term in case its average scholarship for the preceding term falls below the standard required for graduation, was determined upon at an informal faculty-student conference. Different groups of students are called in for consideration of different projects.[1]

Similarly, discovery of student feeling that a given practice is unjust is followed by the appointment of a faculty-student committee to consider the matter. This has led to the removal of misunderstandings and to the correction of actual abuses.

II

The experience thus outlined has, in my opinion, established the validity of the theory of faculty-student co-operation as stated at the beginning of this paper, and has illustrated

[1] The list of qualities indicative of leadership, quoted above, in chapter iv, is the result of a similar co-operative study.

some of the principles necessary for its success and some of the values resulting from such co-operation.

In theory, indeed, such co-operation is indispensable as a phase of educational research. For in any type of research involving conscious beings as objects it is of course of the first importance to obtain full and complete reactions from the objects of the research. By the same token, if we are to understand what college education is actually doing, we must obtain reliable statements of the experience of those who are in the process. Faculty-student co-operation makes this possible both by bringing faculty and students together and by disposing the students toward confidence in the faculty.

One of the formal principles conducive to the success of such co-operation is that when faculty and students thus meet they should be represented in equal numbers. If this is the case no one feels isolated or burdened with an excess of representative responsibility—all are more at ease.[1]

It is of course important that the personnel

[1] I venture to add that I believe this principle of equality of numbers to be helpful also in the matter of the entertainment of students by faculty members. A dinner party, for instance, consisting of one faculty couple and several students or of several faculty couples and one or two students is likely to be badly unbalanced. The most pleasant and successful instances of faculty entertainment of students which I have known have been occasions on which there were just as many students as faculty people present.

of faculty-student groups should be carefully selected. On the faculty side it is particularly important that the men or women chosen be open-minded and ready to see both sides of a question, yet strong with intelligent interest in college education as a whole and able to speak with quiet reasonableness on behalf of their convictions. Students are no more ready than anyone else to accept dogmatic statements unsupported by reasons; students are more ready, in my experience, than the average non-student group to appreciate and be moved by thoughtful argumentation.

The students chosen should in general be upperclassmen,[1] and should of course be men or women respected among their fellows. It is indeed possible that such selection may itself be regarded as an honor. If this situation comes about, selection may well fall at times on students not otherwise "prominent" who because of personal quality deserve encouragement.

Different students should be selected for dif-

[1] I heartily subscribe to the recent statement of Dean Hawkes in his address, "The Liberal Arts College in the University," in the *Amherst Graduates' Quarterly* for February, 1926: "In our American colleges the tendency has been very strong during the last ten years to emphasize a line of cleavage between the first two college years and the last two. . . . . In my experience there is no question that during the first year or two of college life the students are not able to carry completely their responsibilities. They are boys, not men. I am just as clear that juniors and seniors are much better able to carry their responsibilities because for the most part they are men rather than boys."

ferent committees, formal or informal. No occasion should ever be given for thinking of a certain group of students as "yes"-men; and no administrative relation with students should ever be such as to give the slightest basis for suspicion of espionage.

The chief values of faculty-student co-operation have already been suggested. In summary and with some additions they are as follows.

The faculty members stand to gain an understanding, otherwise inaccessible, of the conditions of student life and work, and to benefit in the development of constructive measures of any sort by the sense of general confidence which such co-operation tends to develop. Such an attitude is indeed indispensable if improvements of any sort involving student conduct or tradition are really to "take." If you want to do anything *for* students, do it *with* them—otherwise they think you are doing it *to* them. Administrative officers in particular may have the satisfaction of knowing, in the case of a decision made after co-operation, that students, even though they dislike and disagree with the decision, know that it was reached loyally, and that it is just and desirable in the honest opinion of those who made it.

The students gain whatever values may come from friendly association with older men in investigative and constructive study; a broader and better proportioned knowledge of education as a whole and perhaps of the general social problem; the sense of freedom to suggest and to protest, and the stimulation of creative thought and idealism which comes therewith; and the same sense of general confidence, already alluded to, which should lead to greater satisfaction in many phases of the undergraduate's experience of his college.

I have not attempted to define the range in which such co-operation is applicable. In the work done at Chicago it has dealt in general with matters of social life in the broadest sense, with student activities, or with specific procedures. It has nevertheless touched the essential question of the quality of instruction, and such curricular problems as those represented by the committees on music and on public speaking. I am inclined to believe that the method could well be expanded to the consideration of any problems that are not technically educational or administrative; for I do not fear the admission of students into any committee discussion in which there are justice and clear thinking on the faculty side; and the freshness, even the naïveté, of student opinion is likely to be in general a healthy thing for faculty minds. Even in technical matters I should favor meeting any expressed student interest with full and courteous explanation.

The experience of faculty-student co-operation carries in itself its own immediate reward in the friendly association of older and younger members of the same community; and it has, I believe, possibilities for educational development which we have hardly begun to realize.

VIII

THE COLLEGE BOOKSTORE

Every man has three fields of intellectual experience. The first is the region of his own immediate experience, including the sights he sees with his own eyes, and the sounds he hears with his own ears. This experience is, of course, sharply limited to the years of his own conscious life, and to the space which he inhabits or traverses. The second field is the country, as it were, of the experience of his own companions, made known to him through some form of conversation. Its boundaries in time and space are but little larger than those of the first field. The third field is the well-nigh unlimited world of vicarious experience through books.

The man who has surveyed this world from its mountain-tops, who has beheld its continents, its seas, its rivers, who is acquainted with its men and women, who multiplies his knowledge by the generations and the ages, who is at home and travels well therein, through space and time—that man is an educated man.

It therefore lies at the heart of the college purpose that we persuade and accustom our students to enter and possess the world of

THE COLLEGE BOOKSTORE 109

books, not as transient visitors, but as lifelong and loyal citizens.

The primary instrument of such training is, of course, the college library.

The second instrument of such training is the college bookstore.

And because I believe that the habit of the use of books is so fundamental as a feature and result of college education, I believe that the potential importance of the college bookstore is very great; indeed, far greater than the college has realized.

In one respect, the bookstore has an advantage over the library; for a book read in the library or borrowed from the library cannot yield its message and its treasure so completely, so intimately, as a book that is bought and owned.

How then shall the college bookstore meet its great educational opportunity? Surely by encouraging the habit of the use of books—and that by making the wise ownership of books easily attainable and irresistibly attractive.

That is my text; now for its applications.

The first is a paradox, radical in the extreme—yet I believe it to be practical, sound, and absolutely indispensable for the achieving of the purpose sought. It is this: the college bookstore should be a bookstore. That is, it should be a store for the selling of books, of many books, and of nothing but books. It should not be a store for the selling of stationery, pencils, notebooks, picture postals, pennants, tennis shoes, playing cards, sofa pillows, apples, sweet chocolate, belt buckles, and hairnets. Such things must undoubtedly be sold, but they should not be sold in the bookstore. They are minor accessories; books are major necessities. If you sell your books over one counter in an emporium of odds and ends, you create and reinforce an entirely false sense of the place of books in education and in life. Sell these other things in a general store, or sell them in the college drug store if you prefer; but do not demean your books by putting them in the same farrago. Books are a thing apart.

The bookstore, then, should be a place of books. Not only that, but it should be a place where it is possible, at leisure and in comfort, to examine books. It should approach the character of a private library. It should have shelves, and revolving cases, perhaps, and tables where a few books lie in a normal posture, as if they were comfortable and happy. It should be possible for the visitor to browse. And on the supposition that he might find a book he would like to know a little more about, there should be at least one comfortable chair per thousand students. I do not say that the rugs should be oriental, but there should be rugs—on pleasant afternoons at least. And there should be a practicable fireplace. In short, there should be something of the atmosphere you might hope—

and would probably fail—to find in a place called "Ye Olde Booke Shoppe."

Yet even such an environment would not insure success. For success here, as in every other phase of the college enterprise, depends primarily on personnel. If your books are vended by salesmen to whom they are dead merchandise, they might as well be dead merchandise. If the bookstore is to make reading irresistibly attractive, the books must be ordered, and arranged, and introduced, and talked about, and handled and wrapped up and delivered by men and women who know books and love books deeply and contagiously. This is no task for an illiterate automaton. It is a service akin to that of the professor and the critic, and potentially of equal value. And if these people are to make reading attractive, they must themselves be attractive. They must suggest by their own quality and by their own attitude that good reading is really worth while.

Such a place as I have suggested, presided over by such people, might well become a radiant center of intellectual pleasure and activity. I can imagine that groups with a common literary interest might meet there; and I am certain that professors would be glad to talk from time to time about recent books in the field of general literature or in special fields.

You will see that I have in mind primarily the sale of books other than those required for courses. This is in line with the whole trend of modern college education, which is away from the idea of one book per course. We are stressing collateral reading more and more; and we are striving more and more to achieve an education which is not merely a multiplication of courses, but is a process of mental growth, nourished by reading in many fields—reading which shall supplement and interweave the individual courses. In the store I should not separate the required books from the others. The required book itself should gain in significance and in esteem from such a background.

Clearly, such a store would be more expensive to run than the ordinary store. And it should sell books at the lowest possible prices. For the purpose of such a store would not be to make money, any more than the purpose of the college is to make money. The purpose of such a store would be, indeed, the educative purpose of the college itself. It follows that such a store might properly ask, and receive, a subsidy. And yet I believe that the attractiveness of a store so conducted would very soon render such a subsidy unnecessary.

I will close with a few brief specific suggestions.

The stock should include both new and second-hand books; and among the latter there should always be some old and fine rarities.

Lists of new books, with prices, should be posted frequently, in the library as well as in the bookstore. Members of the faculty and of the library staff might well collaborate in the preparation of such lists.

To students in each course there might well be sent lists of books appropriate for collateral reading in that course, with the price of each.

Textbooks and books appropriate for collateral reading might be rented for a term, instead of sold, for a reasonable fraction of their initial value.

Once or twice a year a general catalogue of special sets or specially priced books should be sent to the entire collegiate body.

A man in charge of such a store might well give advice as to the building up of fraternity libraries.

I have spoken of the store as containing books only. I should include in the term "books" any periodicals that would ultimately be worth binding.

A college bookstore, so conceived and so served, would, I believe, be an educational resource of the highest value, and would leave, in the many students whom it would attract, a strong and permanent influence.

IX

INTERCOLLEGIATE FOOTBALL

I am doubly glad to have the opportunity of addressing the National Collegiate Athletic Association.

In the first place, I consider it an honor to be called into the councils of an organization which has done so much for the improvement of the general character of college sport. College sport is and always will be an integral part of college education. The good which you have done in the realm of college sport has extended, therefore, beyond the limits of the playing field, and has had a good effect upon the general morale of college life.

In the second place, I am thankful to have the opportunity of urging you to cure an unhealthy condition which not only menaces the future of the main intercollegiate sport, but is interfering seriously with the endeavor of the American college to achieve the purpose for which it exists. I am thankful to have the opportunity of urging precisely you to do this, because you are in a better position to take effective curative action than any single institution or than any other national organization.

Intercollegiate football is at the present

time an enormously powerful force in the life of the nation. You have helped to make it so. Every enormously powerful force, if ill directed or undirected, may work great harm. By your salutary actions in the past you have led us to look to you for leadership in the control of football. If, by the extension of your previous policies, you will now adequately control it, you will deserve national gratitude.

Twenty years ago intercollegiate football was on trial because of the dangerousness of the game to the men who played it. You saved the situation.

Today intercollegiate football is again on trial; but this time on a new and still more serious indictment. We are not greatly concerned today with the effect of football upon the men who play the game. Even for them it has its disadvantages, which should be lessened; but for them it has also great advantages, which often do outweigh and might be made generally to outweigh its disadvantages. But the men who play the game are but a tiny fraction— somewhere between 1 and 2 per cent—of the total college population of the country. What happens to any 2 per cent in their college training is, of course, important; but it is obviously far less important than what happens to the 98 per cent. And the new indictment against intercollegiate football is precisely this, that intercollegiate football, as at present conducted, interferes seriously with the education of the

98 per cent—that is, the general mass of undergraduate students.

Suppose it does! What of it? What difference does it make whether the college students of today receive an efficient education or not?

It makes an infinite difference. For the future of the American nation rests primarily with the college students of today. It is, of course, perfectly true that America has numbered and numbers among her leaders men of the richest experience, men of the greatest ability, men of the noblest idealism, who have never been through college. But it is equally and increasingly true that on the whole America derives its leaders, in all fields, from among the graduates of its colleges.

If their leadership is strong, wise, and high-minded, America will prosper. If their leadership is weak, unwise, low-minded, America will decline.

Their leadership will be strong, wise, and high-minded if they receive in college an efficient education. Their leadership will be weak, unwise, or low-minded in proportion as the education which they receive in college is, for any reason whatsoever, inefficient.

The purpose of the American college is to train its students in body, mind, and spirit in such a way as to make them efficient leaders for human society.

Efficient leadership requires, in the first place, a trained body—for only a trained body can stand the exhausting strain of real leadership. A trained body means a body that is not only negatively free from disease but is positively charged with active health.

Efficient leadership requires, in the second place, a trained mind. That means a mind which can analyze a situation; which has or can get the information that will suggest a promising course of action; and which has the persistent energy and the flexibility that will follow that course of action through to a triumphant end.

Efficient leadership requires, most of all, a trained spirit. That means a spirit which is gladly and loyally conscious of the bond that links all men together; a spirit which tests every word and every deed by the test of absolute honesty; a spirit which finds its greatest fulness of life in the enrichment of other life.

If the colleges produce such leadership, they fulfil their purpose. If they do not, they fail. Every element in college life is good or bad just in proportion as it tends to help or tends to thwart the development of such leadership. And every element which by this test proves to be bad must be either cured or cut off.

What is the effect of intercollegiate football as at present conducted upon the training of the general mass of undergraduates in respect to body, mind, and spirit?

There are three ways in which it helps that training. They are set forth as follows in the

"Report on Intercollegiate Football" by Committee G of the American Association of University Professors:

> In the first place it affords a recreation so absorbing as to dispel for the time being whatever mental weariness and anxieties the week may have brought.
>
> In the second place it creates a strong sense of common interest. The sight of the filled stands evokes and intensifies the consciousness of human community, and the sense of the emotional solidarity of each stand, strengthened as each stand participates vicariously in the action of runner or passer or tackler, is in itself a stirring thing. This sense of common interest, continuing throughout the season, tends to develop a common bond of loyalty.
>
> In the third place it affords for the entire football season a clean and interesting topic of conversation and of thought.[1]

These are very real advantages; but in the opinion of the great majority of my colleagues, and in mine, they are far outweighed by the respects in which intercollegiate football interferes with the triple training which the American college seeks to give.

It is not the only thing that so interferes. I would not for a moment place on intercollegiate football the blame for all our shortcomings. And I beg to assure you that college teachers in general and Committee G in particular are deeply and actively concerned with many other

[1] *Bulletin* of the Association, XII (1926), 223.

problems. But the fact remains that in our opinion intercollegiate football as at present conducted interferes to an intolerable degree with the attainment of the purpose of the American college.

The indictment, as formulated in the football report of Committee G, contains five counts. Copies of this report have been sent you recently, and I assume that you have its substance well in mind. In my presentation of the five counts, I shall therefore not repeat the full statements which you will find in the report. I shall review the several counts only briefly, and shall point out in each case how the tendency in question serves to hinder efficient education.

The first count is the overexcitement about football which prevails through the autumn, increasing as the season advances, not limited to the days of the games, infecting more and more of student time and thought, and culminating in the weeks of the big games at the end of the season. This overexcitement manifests itself directly in the neglect of college work, both through the relegation of that work to a position of minor interest and through the actual time taken by prolonged discussions, pep sessions, migrations, and celebrations. This neglect shows itself in absence, in failure to prepare assigned class work, in failure to do collateral reading and to write papers and reports on time, and in inattention in class.

This overexcitement interferes directly with the mental training of the college student, first because it causes him to do a considerable amount of his work poorly or to neglect it altogether; second—and this is a still more serious matter—because it tends, in the early part of the college year, to establish the habit of doing work poorly or not doing it at all—and this habit, once formed, tends to continue throughout the year, particularly after it has been reinforced by the experiences of successive football seasons.

The second count, which is closely related to the first but is still more important and far reaching, is the distortion in the student mind of the normal scale of values of college work and of life. Broadly speaking, the tendency is to think that success in football is more significant and more desirable than any other kind of success. This tendency is greatly increased by publicity of many sorts and by the sheer magnitude of the enormous financial outlay involved in the maintenance of football. It manifests itself among students in the indiscriminate hero-worship of successful players; in the feeling—and in action based thereon—that high-school football players are the most desirable of all possible college freshmen; and, worst of all, in the relative depreciation of less spectacular types of success, and, in particular, in the depreciation of success in college work.

This depreciation of success in college work

shows itself in two ways: first, in lack of esteem or even in something like scorn for those who win distinction in college work; and second, in the tendency to be satisfied, regardless of one's potential ability, with work just good enough to win a passing grade. This distortion of values thus strikes at the very heart of the effort of the college to give mental training to its students— for you cannot give proper mental training to a student who is so unconvinced of the value of what you are trying to do that he will not, on his side, put forth an effort commensurate with his potential ability. And the students of the highest ability, those who are the most likely of all to win positions of outstanding leadership in our national life, are and will be discouraged from the endeavor to attain the full educational development of their ability just so long as distinction in college work rates low in the undergraduate scale of values.

Furthermore, this same distortion of values interferes with the efficient training of the spirit; for it sets up, or reinforces, ideals which are in conflict with those ideals of mutual human service which alone make for the highest type of leadership. If there are two lessons which above all others the American public and, in particular, American youth, need to learn at the present time, they are, first, that publicity is not the ultimate measure of personal significance, and, second, that financial display is not the ultimate measure of success.

And intercollegiate football, as at present conducted, glorifies both publicity and financial display.

The foregoing statements with regard to overexcitement and the distortion of values are made on the basis of long and composite experience in the study of college students. I have myself, in the last three years, talked with more than a thousand college students, individually or in small groups, in Chicago and elsewhere, in such a way as to be able to draw what seem to me reliable conclusions as to the effect of intercollegiate football upon their attitude toward life and work. And my conclusions, based upon this mass of direct human evidence, are confirmed by similar conclusions drawn, upon the basis of similar evidence, by colleagues in many colleges.

Overexcitement and the distortion of values are the main counts in the indictment, and should, by themselves, suffice to call for a thoroughgoing reform. But there are other counts as well, secondary, yet still significant.

One of them, the third count in the series, is the fact that intercollegiate football intensifies the drinking evil—that is, that more than the ordinary amount of drinking takes place before and after football games, particularly among those who are following their teams to games played away from home. Please note that this count, as stated in the Committee G report, and as now repeated, has reference not to the men who play the game but to members of the general non-playing undergraduate body. Please note also that I am not blaming football for the entire drinking evil. I do state that intercollegiate football as at present conducted intensifies the drinking evil; and I further state that any condition which intensifies the drinking evil constitutes a serious interference with the attempt of the colleges to fulfil their educative purpose.

The fourth count is that intercollegiate football games are the object of a considerable amount of betting on the part of undergraduates. This evil is intimately connected with the migration of team followers to other campuses. We are seeking to train our students to base their dealings with other men upon the honest principle that for value received there must be value given. Any practice which tends to create or intensify the habit of getting something for nothing is not only definitely contrary to the educational endeavor, but is obviously subversive of the stability of our national life.

The fifth count is that intercollegiate football as at present conducted, despite the earnest and partially effective and altogether commendable efforts which you have made, is still largely attended, in student opinion and in fact, by the improper financial attraction and maintenance of football players. And so long as students generally believe that players on their own team or on other teams are being surreptitiously financed, just so long the talk of football as a builder of general sportsmanship is a mockery. Suppose the game itself to be played with perfect sportsmanship—what difference does that make when students believe that the very presence of some of the players on the football field is evidence of a hidden and powerful and successful dishonesty which is the antithesis of sportsmanship? And what is the effect of this belief upon the endeavor of the colleges to produce leaders who will base their leadership on honesty?

The five counts I have mentioned are the five main counts brought forward in the report of Committee G with reference to the effect of football upon the undergraduate body as a whole.

If you need more, read the rest of that report; or read indictments other than this. For this indictment does not stand alone. It is but one in an increasing series uttered not only by men who are devoting their lives to the task of higher education—and who may therefore be dismissed as biased when they speak in defense of their life work!—but by thoughtful publicists, and even by undergraduates conscious that they are being thwarted in the high adventure of the educational quest.

That is the situation. What will you do about it?

Every one of the charges I have brought is concerned, directly or indirectly, with the overexcitement produced by the game as at present conducted. That overexcitement, in turn, is due primarily to two causes: first, the intense desire for teams so expert that they may be confidently expected to defeat their rivals, and second, the glare of publicity—in the college community itself, in every larger community which the students touch, and most of all in the daily press—which beats upon the head of the individual football player. These two causes are back of the overexcitement in general, and they are directly and obviously back of the surreptitious financial maintenance of football players.

Any remedy which is to be effective must correct these two causes. That remedy will be best which will correct these two causes most effectively and at the same time interfere least with the benefits of the game. That remedy will be ideal which, while correcting these two causes, will at the same time extend the benefits of the game.

Five different remedial plans have been proposed; and I shall now, in closing, briefly review these five plans. They are the one-year plan, the two-year plan, the four-game plan, the class-team plan, and the double-team plan.

The first, which is, I believe, by far the best, was suggested by one of your own members, Dr. Edgar Fauver, of Wesleyan University. It is simply this, that no man should be allowed to engage in intercollegiate competition in a given sport for more than one season. This plan would serve admirably to correct the two underlying causes of the overexcitement. For the annual shift in playing personnel would make constant expectation of a winning team impossible, and would do away very largely with excessive individual publicity—since such publicity is almost entirely concerned with players who are in their second or third year of performance. Furthermore, it would strike directly and effectively at the surreptitious maintenance of football players. For even the men who now participate in the surreptitious maintenance of football players would hesitate to finance for several years a man who could compete in only one year. And the Fauver plan not only corrects the evils I have listed, but definitely extends the advantages of the game; for it multiplies by three the number of men engaging in intercollegiate competition and receiving therefrom those benefits in respect to training in discipline, training in co-operation, and coming under the personal influence of the coach, which you will find set forth in the report of Committee G.

Of the other four plans, every one would alleviate the present situation, but no one, in my opinion, is so thoroughgoing as to give promise of effecting a cure.

The two-year plan is similar in tendency to the one-year plan, but is obviously less effective, both in its correction of evils and in its extension of benefits. It has two forms. The first, proposed at the 1925 meeting of this association by Dr. Wilce, of Ohio State University, is to the effect that competition should be limited to the junior and senior years. This would act to reduce the surreptitious maintenance of football players; but I do not think that it would greatly lessen either the confident expectation of a winning team or the amount of publicity beating upon the individual player. Nor would it greatly increase the number of men engaging in intercollegiate competition. The second form of the plan, proposed in 1925 by Arthur Howe and again in 1926 by the Special Committee on Athletics of the Ohio College Association, is to the effect that competition should be limited to the sophomore and junior years. This would not act so effectively to reduce the surreptitious maintenance of football players, but it seems to me superior in every other respect to the first form of the plan. It would also fall in with the increasing feeling that a senior ought to be free to devote himself to final preparation for the serious business of life, which is for him so soon to begin.

The four-game plan was advanced in 1925 at the Wesleyan Undergraduate Parley. It would help to some extent; but if the same men are allowed to play for three years I do not believe that either the confident expectation of a winning team or the publicity centering on individual stars would be greatly decreased. If the total length of the season were to be what it is at present, I do not think that the reduction in the number of games would make much difference. If, however, the total length of the season from the time the men first report to the day of the final game should be limited to, say, six weeks, there would be a decided corrective gain. On the other hand, this plan is inferior to the two preceding plans in that it does not increase at all the total number of men engaged in intercollegiate competition; and in that it would unduly limit the number of outdoor Saturday afternoon entertainments for the college community.

The class-team plan has not, I think, been publicly presented hitherto. It originates with Professor Pyre, of Wisconsin, and is to the effect that there should be no varsity team but that class teams should be allowed to play intercollegiate games—the sophomore team perhaps two games, the junior team perhaps three games, and the senior team perhaps four games. This plan has corrective value and would increase the number of men receiving the experience of intercollegiate competition. But it seems to me that it would be difficult to administer, and that it puts too much stress on playing in the senior year. And I do not believe that the American college will ever be content with an athletic system which does not culminate in a varsity team.

INTERCOLLEGIATE FOOTBALL

The double-team plan has been advocated, I believe, by President Little, of the University of Michigan. The essence of this plan is that each college should have two varsity teams, and that when College A plays College B there should be two games, one at A and one at B. This plan has the advantage of increasing the number of men engaged in intercollegiate competition. It would do away almost entirely with football migration, and would consequently diminish the great evils now connected with that migration; but it does not give promise of an effective cure for the other and still greater evils.

You have before you, gentlemen, the opportunity to make a decision momentous not only for the future of the game you love, but for the future of the American college, which I hope and believe you love still more.

You have maintained, and I have maintained, that one of the greatest benefits which intercollegiate football gives to the men who play it is training in co-operation—the subordination of individual interest to the good of the whole team. You, as the representatives of collegiate athletics, constitute, in a sense, a single member of that truly all-American college team on which the rest of us are playing too. We are not playing to defeat friendly rivals; we are playing to defeat all the forces of weakness, of ignorance, of inefficiency, of selfishness, and of dishonesty which beset the American nation, and to win new strength, new wisdom, new power, new brotherliness, new standards of honor, new fulness of life. It is the greatest game in the world today. Won't you play the game with us—and help us win?

NOTE

The essay on "The Changing College" appeared in the "Educational Supplement" of the *New Republic* for April 14, 1926. As there printed, it carried footnotes referring to various reports by Committee G of the American Association of University Professors, and to President Aydelotte's report on honors courses, published by the National Research Council.

The second and third essays were written for a forthcoming co-operative volume on *The Organization and Administration of Higher Education*, edited by Dean R. A. Kent. Much of the material of the third essay will be used in my inaugural address as President of Oberlin College, to be delivered in October, 1927.

The address, hitherto unpublished, entitled "Who Shall Go to College?" was delivered at a joint meeting of the Parent-Teacher Associations of the Lincoln School and the Horace Mann School in March, 1927.

The narrative of my interview with the blind freshman has been used in substance in a number of addresses delivered to local alumni associations of the University of Chicago, but has not hitherto been published in its present form. The student in question graduated from the University of Chicago, with high honors, in June, 1927.

The article on "Freshman Week" was published in the *School Review* for December, 1924.

The paper on "Faculty-Student Co-operation"

was published in the *Bulletin* of the Association of American Colleges for May, 1926.

The talk on "The College Bookstore" was given in June, 1925, to a gathering of managers of college bookstores, and was published, under the title "The College Bookstore as an Educational Resource," in the *Publishers' Weekly* for July 25, 1925.

The address on "Intercollegiate Football" was delivered on December 30, 1926, at the annual meeting of the National Collegiate Athletic Association, and was published, under the title "The Relation of Intercollegiate Football to the Purpose of the American College," in the *Proceedings* of that Association for 1926, and in *School and Society* for February 5, 1927.

All of the essays and addresses here reprinted have been slightly modified in preparation for publication in this book.

〚 PRINTED IN U·S·A· 〛